TO INFINITY
AND BEYOND

S0-ABC-281

Steve Holmes is an ex-punk whose band once supported the Boomtown Rats. The anarchy may have died but his adventurous spirit remains. Steve got into two wheels via a Lambretta SX200 but nowadays rides a Ducati 749s so you could say his experience of bikes is diverse. Even so, the Norton 500 took some getting used to. So far Steve's South American experiences have not led him to start any revolutions in his hometown of Blackburn, Lancashire.

TO INFINITY AND BEYOND

What Che Guevara started,
someone had to finish

Stephen E. Holmes

Copyright © Stephen E. Holmes, 2011
The right of Stephen Holmes to be identified as the author of this
book has been asserted in accordance with the Copyright, Designs
and Patents Act 1988.

First published in 2011 by
Infinite Ideas Limited
36 St Giles
Oxford
OX1 3LD
United Kingdom
www.infideas.com

All rights reserved. Except for the quotation of small passages for the
purposes of criticism or review, no part of this publication may be
reproduced, stored in a retrieval system or transmitted in any form or
by any means, electronic, mechanical, photocopying, recording, scan-
ning or otherwise, except under the terms of the Copyright, Designs
and Patents Act 1988 or under the terms of a licence issued by the
Copyright Licensing Agency Ltd, 90 Tottenham Court Road, London
W1T 4LP, UK, without the permission in writing of the publisher.
Requests to the publisher should be addressed to the Permissions
Department, Infinite Ideas Limited, 36 St Giles, Oxford, OX1 3LD,
UK, or faxed to +44 (0) 1865 514777.

A CIP catalogue record for this book is available from the British
Library

ISBN 978–1–906821–90–6

Brand and product names are trademarks or registered trademarks of
their respective owners.

Cover designed by Vanessa Dean, Richards Bay, South Africa
Text designed and typeset by Nicki Averill
Photographs by Pete Sandford and Steve Holmes
Printed and bound in Great Britain

Contents

Acknowledgements

Without Pete Sandford's foresight and dreams this adventure would never have taken place. I am pleased and proud that he asked me along and that we successfully completed the journey for Che and Alberto.

Thanks to Richard Burton from Infinite Ideas for taking the time to read my manuscript, having faith in me and buying me lunch!

There are a few people without whom I wouldn't have put pen to paper or indeed carried on writing when I had doubts about this chronicle. Lynne Jackson and her father who started me off and Alan and Jo Varney, Sheila Shaw, Margaret Crane and Vanessa Dean who all showed faith and willed me to the finish line.

I am deeply indebted to everybody whose name is mentioned in this book and would like to thank you all very much. Thanks also to those whose names aren't mentioned but who helped along the way, and to the endless list of people I encountered on the road.

Sandra Heker, Javier Kaper, Karl-Heinz Pfarr, Fabrizio Tapia, Gustavo Agra, Alejandro Tolosana, Mariana Lucía Sammarco, Mariana Guadalupe Maceddo and her friend Rosana all showed us the wonderful hospitality and warmth that the Argentinian people should be proud of.

Chuck Weaver and Goose from Texas were on their own adventure and looked after us in Buenos Aires.

Isabel Bussenius, Paula Cattan Castillo and Ricardo Adrian Zamora Vergera at La Casona 1920 de Iquique and Ivan and Silvia in Santiago made Chile a wonderful place.

Jeff, his wife Yahira, Glen Short and Jolanda van den Berg made our stay in Cusco special and Gustavo and his brother Alejandro from Ica helped us when we eventually got out of the sandstorm.

The *aduana* in Colombia got us through customs with no problems.

Migdalia at the Swissport cargo office in Caracas airport got the bikes back home. And thanks to President Hugo Chavez for cheap beer and even cheaper fuel.

If I haven't mentioned your name it is not intentional, we met so many wonderful people on our adventure. The last thank you I have saved for the South American people as a whole, who showed us nothing but warmth and generous hospitality wherever we went.

Introduction

I first met Pete Sandford in 1977 during the rebellious, bored teenager years of punk rock. I was an 18 year old with an attitude and a will to be at the forefront of the anarchy that the youth of that day believed in. The days of the Sex Pistols, The Clash and a band called Demolition, which I formed with Pete! We mostly played at local venues round our home town of Blackburn. The highlights were supporting the Boomtown Rats (led by a certain Bob Geldof), and playing live in front of 3,500 people at a Rock against Racism gig in Wigan. In those days anarchy was expressed through music and song.

I guess our first adventure together was a lads' holiday in Newquay. I use the word adventure because we did the whole 700-mile round trip in a beaten-up Volkswagen Beetle that was belching more carbon monoxide into the passenger compartment than could possibly have been coming out of the exhaust pipe. Consequently, we had to do the whole trip with all the windows open and, thanks to the ever reliable British weather, it rained for the whole journey. Drenched, excited, tired and with throats like your average 50-a-day smoker, we eventually arrived in Newquay more in need of an oxygen tent than the four-man tent we were to sleep in.

I lost contact with Pete in the early 1980s as we went our separate ways. He pursued his rebellion by teaching windsurfing in France. I was on a mission to carry on the anarchy by becoming a scooter boy with a job in the local aircraft building industry.

Strangely, it was punk rock which brought us back together about 30 years later. A local lad was at a punk festival when Demolition came up. I was contacted and it brought memories of the heady days of my youth flooding back. I managed to get hold of Pete via his mother, who thankfully hadn't moved from the same village she had always lived in. We found we weren't close neighbours – Pete lived on Hayling Island in Hampshire where his windsurfing business had taken him with his wife Michelle and I, being the home-bird, still lived in Blackburn, Lancashire. We hooked up for a meal and a lot of catching up. The conversation turned to motorcycles, a passion we both shared, and how it would be a fantastic experience to tour Europe together.

We kept in touch throughout 2007 with the odd e-mail, until Pete's idea was suggested in a message on 7th February, 2008.

I've got to admit that when I first received Pete's e-mail asking me to do the trip with him I was more than a little apprehensive. The idea came out of Pete sitting at home watching a movie. We both got a little carried away with ideas including a TV series, a book and a DVD, but the dream quickly escalated into reality. At first we just wanted to see how far we would get on the old Nortons. I don't think for one moment that either of us believed we would complete the whole trip through the vast continent and I don't think anybody else did either.

The trip totally changed my outlook on life and I can now see why it changed the attitude of the two young Argentinian doctors back in 1952. The five capital cities of the countries we passed through are like any modern cities in the world, but they mask the endemic poverty that is rife in all five countries. Very little has changed since Ernesto 'Che' Guevara and Alberto Granado visited and without getting political, it is hard to not feel humbled by the plight of the poor and needy in these countries. Argentina, Chile, Peru, Colombia and Venezuela all have vast mineral, agricultural and oil resources, yet the wealth these industries generate does not reflect in the standard of living of the Latin American people, their infrastructure or their towns and villages.

To spend 24 hours a day, 7 days a week with someone, you really do need to get on with the person. Pete and I are totally different but, as it turned out, perfect together. If we had been of similar character we would still be drinking beer in Buenos Aires now. What started off as a road trip quickly turned into an adventure as we battled through the adverse elements of the roads, the weather and the landscape. I quickly learned that you can truly adapt to any conditions in your surroundings, including lots of urine-stained mattresses! Sleeping rough under the bright starlight was almost romantic and the friendliness and hospitality we received throughout Latin America will truly live with me forever. When you see the smiles on the faces of the very poor you realise that the important things in life truly are the simple things you take for granted, your family and friends.

My fondest memories of our little adventure are definitely the beautiful sunsets we witnessed every day as we rode the bikes through that vast continent. Foundation Niños Unidos Peruanos in Cusco where Jolanda van den Berg and her staff feed over 600 Peruvian children every day reduced me to tears of sadness and joy and was the real highlight of the trip. My worst memory is undoubtedly the night we nearly perished on a mountain in Peru, when the kindness of a South American 'from Ipswich' and Lady Luck probably saved our lives

The journey was possibly the hardest thing I have done in my life, but I look back with pride at what we both achieved. Thanks to Pete's mechanical know-how and a hell of a lot of luck we both came through the ordeal unscathed and better people. My only regret? That the wonderful adventure had to come to an end, because I felt I could have ridden on forever.

Caracas

Venezuela

Guyana · French Guiana

Colombia · Suriname

Ecuador

Peru

Brazil

Bolivia

Paraguay

Chile

Argentina

Uraguay

Buenos Aires

South America

Chapter I
Making a plan

Steve, have you seen The Motorcycle Diaries? *About a young Che Guevara and his mate touring round South America on a 1939 Norton 500? Well, wouldn't it be fantastic to recreate the journey on the exact same model of bike, hopefully starting Jan 2009. It's going to take about eight weeks, starting in Buenos Aires, Argentina & ending in the north of Peru, 10,000 miles later.*

It's early days yet and I'm still doing lots of reading & planning but I reckon this could be THE trip that we were talking about when we last met up. With that in mind I think it'll be best if we do the trip, either both on old Nortons or one riding a modern bike (Kawa 650 or similar). So – the question is – how about it? Will she let you out for eight weeks next Jan? That's if you still fancy it? I think we'd have a great laugh, in-between all the puncture repairs & breakdowns and it'll be a real low budget trip. Apart from shipping the bikes over by sea there won't be much to spend on. I've still not broken this news to Michelle (the wife) yet so if you call at the weekend & speak to her don't mention it yet. That said, I nearly bought a Norton last week so I'll have to break the news soon!!

Speak soon ok? Cheers, Pete

As I read the e-mail I must admit I took it rather lightly as I am not your average Dr Livingstone and have never been much of an adventure seeker. Although I had done the world's highest bungee jump if that counts? First, I had definitely not seen *The Motorcycle Diaries*, or even heard of it for that matter. I only knew of Che Guevara from seeing his image on T-shirts and because David Bowie mentioned him in his song *Panic in Detroit*. As for doing it on an old Norton 500! Eight weeks off work? My head was spinning!

I had only recently watched *The Long Way Round*, a brilliant round the world motorcycle documentary starring Ewan McGregor and Charley Boorman. With no disrespect to them, they had done it on brand new BMW motorcycles straight out of the crate, had scores of people to sort out their every need including pick-up trucks, a whole film crew, technicians and more back-up than the Japanese at Pearl Harbor. They were on a package holiday compared to what Pete was suggesting we do.

There was no question that if we were going to do this we would do it the right way, no Kawa KLR 650 or similar, and certainly not a brand new BMW. This would have to be true to the trip taken by a 23-year-old Ernesto 'Che' Guevara and his 29-year-old friend Alberto Granado back in January 1952, on a Norton 500 motorcycle named *La Poderosa II* (The Mighty One). This adventure would be attempted on two Norton 500cc motorcycles, of which only 100,000 were supplied to the British Army during World War II. That just left us the small problem of finding two of them.

I was a scooter boy back in the early 1980s and it was during this time that I fell in love with the thrill of riding on two wheels. With the wind against your face and the freedom, there is nothing quite like it. As I have gotten older I have found that owning a motorcycle in whatever shape or form is like being a member of a secret society. You are drawn to other members of this secret club. You talk about your experiences, your thrills and spills, the mechanical breakdowns, parts and even the little tweaks you have given your machine. That is because they understand what you are talking about, because in this secret club even strangers are friends. They have shared the same or similar experiences and they talk in the same language, which always mentions their beloved 'wheels'. Just try talking to someone outside this inner circle, someone who has never ridden on two wheels. They will probably yawn as their glass eye falls slowly to sleep! They will never know what it is like to accelerate like the wind up to speeds of 170 mph and beyond. They will never know what it is like to have a grin hidden behind your visor. They will never know the freedom, the camaraderie, or the adrenalin rush you can only ever get by being a member of the hidden world of motorcycling.

I myself had to put the question of making the trip to my fiancée, Mandie. We were to marry in May 2008, and here I was planning to be gone for two months before we even hit our first wedding anniversary. I had met Mandie through our shared passion for motorcycles. I was on my way back from a motorcycling weekend in Fort William, Scotland with some friends on my Ducati 749s. I absolutely love this bike. When I am riding her man and machine are one! Mandie was on her equally beloved Gixer 600. She whipped past my friends and I at about warp factor 2 leaving me thinking, 'God, he's in a hurry.' We arrived at the next service area on the motorway to find that this biker in a hurry was female. I won't go into details, but needless to say a lot of you will have met your wives over a gallon of Stella Artois, I met mine over a gallon of unleaded.

Chapter 2
Twice bitten

Pete is the kind of guy who, if he fell off a men's outfitters roof, would land in a three-piece suit. Within a week he had located a Norton 500. How did the world function or do its locating of artefacts before eBay?

Pete picked the Norton up for £2,850 – a snip. It was in original condition and had only 29,000 miles on the clock, although it did require some attention. Soon after, the Norton club, where Pete had placed a classified advertisement, contacted him to say they had a member who was selling one – fully restored and in absolutely mint condition. Would he be willing to pay £2,500 for it? It was a done deal before the gentleman who was selling it had managed to get the words out of his mouth. Pete was now the proud owner of two Nortons!

I showed Mandie the e-mail that Pete had sent, hoping it would serve as a bit of back-up to the question I was about to pose to her. But before I could finish asking how she felt about me going, she was telling me that it would be the adventure of a lifetime and that at 49 years old I wouldn't get many more opportunities to do something like it (that stung a bit, because in my head I am still about 18!). She was right though: how often would I get to walk the Inca trail and to follow in the footsteps of Che Guevara on the route that was to mould him into the revolutionary he became, that moulded the future of Cuba? It was indeed a chance I had to grasp with both hands.

I rang Pete to tell him the news. In my mind I was 70 per cent sure I was going, but it was now June 2008 and I hadn't got a bike or indeed any idea of our aims, the route we would be taking or about the two young Argentinians, Ernesto and Alberto. They had set out on the trip over half a century ago (even before *I* was born) and hadn't made it on a 13-year-old Norton. What chance did Pete and I stand on Nortons that were over 60 years old?

I thought it would be a good idea if I watched *The Motorcycle Diaries* and read the book. It was written from diaries Ernesto and Alberto had kept during the six months it took them to complete their journey: by motorcycle as far as Santiago in Chile and the rest of the way on foot and hitch-hiking. I enjoyed the film about the adventures of the two young men, and could only admire them as they experienced its ups and downs.

I suggested to Pete that I buy the first Norton he had bought and he was only too happy to oblige. Now we had a Norton each but we needed to make a plan and get our act together as we only had six months before our departure. I had to make a trip to Pete's home at Hayling Island to see my steed, my Norton 500.

I set off for Hayling Island at 4 a.m. on 23rd June, 2008. Our plan was to make a short film of Pete and myself riding the Nortons to put on a website, with the aim of getting some sponsorship for shipping the motorcycles out to Buenos Aires. I duly arrived at about 9.30 a.m. to a warm welcome from my old friend. There was torrential rain outside but we were confident it would clear up enough to enable us to strut our stuff in front of Pete's camcorder.

It cleared up around noon, by which time we had watched a couple of episodes of *The Long Way Round* to get us in the mood and give us some idea of what was ahead of us. Did we need a Macedonian interpreter? Or indeed terrorist training? I didn't like the thought of being held captive after being kidnapped by some

Colombian drug cartel in Bogotá on the final leg of our journey. Perhaps we should have self-defence training? Although I have yet to see a karate chop stand up to an AK47 assault rifle.

Then, I finally got to meet the friend I was to ride for the two months we would be together in Latin America. Pete's gleaming Norton sat in his double garage looking absolutely pristine, like it had just rolled off the production line at the factory founded by James Lansdowne Norton all those years ago. The bike was wheeled out into the overcast, now greying skies of Hampshire and rested on its centre stand. The petrol taps were opened and as the Amal carburettor was tickled Pete let off some compression via the lever on the handlebar and the 4.9:1 compression engine kicked into life. After a little cough and throat-clearing, the 500cc engine peaked and sounded as sweet as a cathedral chorister hitting a top C. Wow, I thought to myself, this is really going to happen – Pete was going to make it happen. After a couple of turns on the twist grip throttle she settled down to tick over like a Lancaster bomber running on one engine, sounding as sweet as a nut! Next it was the turn of the Norton stuck away in the corner of the garage. From the back I could just make out the black and white number plate KOP 27.We got her out onto the drive next to the other Norton. They were like twins that had been separated at birth. Mine looked like the one brought up by foster parents on a rather rough council estate, never having had the love and tender care it so rightly deserved. Pete's Norton was the twin that had been given the silver spoon treatment from birth, its every whim and cry catered for. His bike had grown into a prince, mine was the pauper.

But I liked her. She was just as I had imagined, true to her roots and totally original. Everything, with the exception of the tyres was what she had left the factory with. She was what had made British motorcycles the envy of the world! As Pete gave her the same gentle tickle he had given his own machine, KOP 27 popped and burst into life, singing from the same hymn sheet as the bike next to her.

We decided to take the bikes to the end of the lane, an intrepid journey of about half a mile. The first thing I had to get used to was the gearing and the rear brakes. On the majority of modern bikes the gear lever is situated on the left side of the bike and the brake lever is on the right side, both foot operated. To add to the confusion the gearing on my Ducati is one 'down' and five 'up' whereas the Norton is one 'up' and three 'down'. Making the change between modern and historic bikes is a little like rubbing your tummy and patting your head! We set off in tandem, accelerating down the lane. I had to look down at the gears as I had never ridden anything like this before. As we neared the end of the lane, I squeezed on the front brake lever and put my right foot on what I thought was the rear brake lever (in reality the gear lever). 'Oh no this is it!' I thought as the bike continued towards the junction with no intention of stopping on the front brake alone. Suddenly my left foot seemed to develop a mind of its own and pushed down hard on the rear brake lever, bringing me to an abrupt halt before I was side-swiped by one of our four wheeled adversaries. Almost immediately the engine stalled and gave up the ghost. She wouldn't respond to the kick-over she was getting and we were left with no option but to tow her back to Pete's garage. Using all his technical wizardry Pete decided to pull out the saviour of British bikes: the plug spanner.

With a change of plug (borrowed from Pete's son's go-kart) my Norton was given the kiss of life and after a short cough and a little spurt was kicked back into action. It was time to make our short film on Hayling Island beach.

Realising that we couldn't film the two of us riding side-by-side and move the camcorder at the same time Pete rang Chas, an elderly neighbour with no previous experience of camcorders or filming. 'How do you switch the bloody thing on?' he asked. I was in a borrowed leather jacket, jeans and an open face helmet. For the filming I was to wear a leather flying hat with goggles to give a 1950s look, a bit like Clark Gable. But without the moustache, smouldering good looks and panache I looked like a flying pig!

We set off to the beach, about a mile and a half away from the house. The Nortons growled up the road, turning heads and setting off car alarms as the drone of the single piston shook the ground beneath us. I was smiling like a lottery winner – they really are a joy to ride.

We would be filming about half a mile down the beach, so we headed down the shale on the bikes, leaving our intrepid cameraman to walk after us. Riding down was difficult in places as the weight and torque of the Norton dug deep into the shale at times, but the brutish Brit never let up, leaving a furrow like a farmer's freshly ploughed field behind us.

The view out to sea was quite spectacular. In front of us, looking out across the Solent was the Isle of Wight, which I had never seen before. The string of container ships in the foreground seemed to be strung together like a necklace. Glittering sunlight somehow managed to penetrate the gloomy clouds above. For me the adventure had started. If I was 70 per cent convinced before I came to Hayling that I was going, then that day on the beach grasped the romantic in me. Looking out to sea, riding the Norton on the beach and feeling all nostalgic, I had hit the 100 per cent mark. Argentina, Chile, Peru, Colombia and Venezuela: here I come!

As we parked the bikes to wait for our cameraman a coastguard approached us to tell us that motorcycles were not allowed on the beach. We explained that we were making a short film about the trip, and seeing the vintage British motorcycles and realising we weren't there to tear up the beach, he allowed us to carry on. He went back to let his controlled explosive off on the rogue flare that had washed ashore, and we continued to wait, and wait.

Eventually Chas appeared. We showed him how to work the camera, climbed on our bikes and ... the heavens opened and the rain came lashing down! We couldn't see the Isle of Wight; in fact we couldn't see anything. It was like a monsoon! I let out a short burst of laughter as I looked at our cameraman getting soaked trying to raise a trot to hasten his half mile journey back to the car, but as they say, 'he who laughs last...' I ran to my bike and kicked it, and kicked it. Nothing – absolutely nothing. Pete was having the same reaction from his bike too. We looked at each other and made for the sand dunes to try to take shelter. When the rain let up a little we had the arduous task of pushing the bikes back along the beach. It was sheer hard graft as they sank in the dunes and shale. It seemed to take an eternity to get to the beach car park as the driving rain came back at us, and we still had a mile and a half to push the bikes back to Pete's. Chas was probably back at his house by now drying himself and having a chuckle at our predicament. I could see now why Japanese bikes became so popular.

The following morning we woke up to sunlight aplenty and new hope. We fitted new spark plugs and headed for the beach. Today was what we had been waiting for. Lights, camera, action! But alas, no Chas. We decided to set the camera up and just ride past it a couple of times.

It was in the can! As we were leaving the beach that day, my bike seemed a little wobbly. We got to the pub for some lunch, only to discover a rear puncture. Not bad: I had managed to ride the Norton a total of six miles, had pushed it for two of those, towed it for half a mile, broken down twice, and had a puncture. Roll on the 10,000 mile trek, it should be a doddle!

My next mission was to kit myself out. The riding leathers, Arai helmet and Sidi boots I owned would look totally out of place on the old Norton. So I turned to that reliable online auction site again. What I needed to look the part was something waterproof, with a little body armour and a 'pisspot' helmet with goggles. I acquired a Belstaff jacket and some riding trousers, all brand new, but they looked right. I also bid on and won some Royal Enfield saddlebags which looked perfect in the pictures. When they arrived, they did look the part, but whoever wrote the item description must have got centimetres and inches mixed up because they wouldn't hold a packed lunch, never mind two months' worth of clothing, cameras etc. It was back to the old drawing board. I needed panniers that would hold my hair straighteners, hair dryer, Brylcreem and factor 50 sun cream. Hey, we were going to shoot the whole thing on high definition cameras, I'd have to look my best at all times! I finally settled for some leather saddlebags the same as Pete's. They were large enough to hold the camcorders, cameras, the spares we would need to carry with us, and possibly, at a squeeze, a couple of T-shirts. Gone was the idea that I would be able to take a clean pair of underpants for every day of the week.

Pete e-mailed me a couple of weeks later to tell me that he'd sourced another Norton 500 that was to be sold at a motorcycle auction in Southport and that I would probably get a bargain.

I have been a little wary of buying anything motorised from an auction ever since the day in 1976 when I attended a motor auction in Blackburn and immediately fell in love with a gleaming purple Ford Corsair. That was in the days of 'bought as seen'. The bidding started at £7.00, I joined in at about £15.00 and up it went in one pound stages, my arm went up three times and at £25.50 I owned the car of my dreams. The dream quickly turned into a nightmare. After paying and receiving the log book and keys I walked over to her (the friend who was with me was green with envy as two weeks previously he had purchased an MG for £30.00 that was rotten as a carrot). I sat in the Corsair and I was like a pea in a drum – it was a very spacious car inside. I felt like I'd got an absolute bargain until I pulled out onto the open road. I selected first gear and as the two litre engine purred like a Serengeti lion, I went for second gear, only to discover that first gear was the only forward gear the car possessed. It was to prove a very costly purchase.

I arrived at the motorcycle auction in Southport, along with my friend Adam, at around lunchtime, giving us time to have a viewing, get a feel for the place and get a bidding number. We had a quick look round at the various ancient and modern two-wheeled flights of fantasy on offer. There were some very clean models about, but farmers must own the majority of old motorcycles in Britain as many were what the auctioneer described as 'barn finds'. Quite why so many people had suddenly discovered an old motorcycle in their barn was beyond me. But these rusting relics of British greatness were here in force, mainly held together by green mould and moss. Still, one man's junk is another man's treasure, as I was to find out later.

The Norton was in reasonable condition, although it hadn't run for four years. I knew that this was the bike that would share my pain and joy as I attempted to ride her through South America. Lot 62, Norton 500 16H, first registered in 1937 with two careful owners (and three reckless ones) in standard black and silver. It was a lot cleaner than KOP 27 (the Norton at Pete's), and the 16H was Norton's pre-war workhorse. Its 500cc side valve engine produced only 16 hp but the ultra-low compression meant it would run on anything vaguely connected to petroleum, which sounded a big plus if the Andean leper colony in Peru ran a bit short of four-star. I thought it had the same spec as Alberto's bike. The guide price was £2,500–£2,800. I set a budget of three grand for myself and decided to see if Pete was right and I could grab myself a bargain.

We had a bit of time in hand so, on Adam's suggestion, we headed for the pub, hoping that a couple of pints would relax me so I wouldn't scratch my nose at the wrong time during the auction and end up finding myself the owner of a 'barn find'.

After our liquid lunch we returned to the auction. Very few of the lots seemed to be reaching their guide prices; it did look as though I was in for a bargain. The bidding was opened for the Norton by a telephone bidder who started at £2,700. This wasn't my day! My hand only went up once and I owned Lot 62 for £3,190. It was the only motorcycle that went over its guide price that day. But I felt a tinge of excitement at owning the old campaigner – this bike was 71 years old and was in great nick.

When I picked the bike up a week later, I couldn't wait to see if she would run. Although it hadn't run for four years friends, including Pete, assured me that it wasn't rocket science and that all I needed was a gallon of petrol and a spark plug. My toolkit at home consists of two hammers and a 10 mm spanner, not exactly equipment to start tinkering with a 71-year-old British bike. A trip to Halfords to get a spark plug spanner and a petrol can was all that was needed. As I put the petrol nozzle into my newly purchased petrol can and pulled the trigger, I got covered in unleaded. As hard as I tried I couldn't stop the petrol blowing back at me. It had registered as £2.30 on the pump, but in truth I bet there wasn't 30 pence worth of petrol in the plastic container. 'What a bad design,' I thought before realising that the can had its nozzle screwed into the receptor. After undoing this I managed to fill the can to its brim quite easily, although the petrol station attendant was curious as to how I had fitted two gallons of petrol into a one gallon container. It was everywhere.

When I got home I pulled the Norton onto level ground at the side of my house and introduced it to my new plug spanner. Well, that was as far as it got as the plug spanner wouldn't fit underneath the tank and onto the spark plug. Fortunately the existing spark plug was only finger tight in the cylinder head so I removed it and replaced it with the brand new plug, tightening it up with my fingers. I then screwed the inner nozzle onto the petrol can and gave the Norton her first drink of petrol in four years. The tank accepted the full gallon with room to spare. I had spilled a little, so I went into the kitchen and got a pan full of water to swill the driveway down so the fuel wouldn't burn through the newly sealed concrete imprinted surface. Still the petrol cascaded from the tank. I looked up and noticed a steady stream of fuel running from a hole in the bottom of the tank. There was only one thing for it, I'd have to catch the petrol in the pan. After wrecking two pans and burning a white patch on my driveway I was thoroughly cheesed off. There was only one thing for it: I rented a van, put the Norton in the back and set off for Hayling Island.

Pete and I took the Norton from the back of the hire van and wheeled it to his garage where the other two

Nortons seemed to be waiting to be joined by a long lost brother.

I explained the problems I'd had in trying to get the bike running. Pete took one look at the bike, and then looked at me. 'Steve, all the oil pipes are disconnected. If you had succeeded in getting it started you would have blown the bloody thing up!' I realised then that even if I purchased a Haynes manual and read it from front to back, it would make as much sense to me as if I attempted to read the Bible in Hebrew! I wasn't cut out for tinkering with a combustion engine. This was a job for our mechanic, Pete.

After a light lunch of eggs, eggs and more eggs (Pete and Michelle keep hens), we decided to draw up a list of what we would need for the journey, have a look at maps of where we would be going, and look on the internet at the Foreign Office's opinion on each country we would be passing through for visas, vaccinations and safety.

Argentina was fine, we studied the route we would be taking, starting from Buenos Aires heading south towards Patagonia before heading west and crossing the Andes into Chile. We would then ride the full length of Chile, passing through the driest place on the planet, the Atacama Desert (I made a mental note to carry extra Perrier water and a spare gallon of fuel – I didn't want to end up on a buzzard's banqueting table). We would then cross into Peru heading towards Cusco and ride what is said to be the most beautiful road in the world to Ollantaytambo and the old Inca city of Machu Picchu. As I was fingering the route on the map it seemed so easy, ride from this place onto the next, then the next. The fact was – we wouldn't be on brand new motorcycles. Then again, what sort of fun would it be on a new bike?

The Foreign Office advice was good until we crossed the border from Peru into Colombia. There the advice was: Do NOT travel to Colombia unless your journey is absolutely necessary! Well, it was necessary if we were to complete our journey and finish in the capital of Venezuela, Caracas. Where we have express takeaways and express pizza delivery, apparently in Colombia they have express kidnappings, especially of foreigners and foreign tourists! This was quite a worry. Apart from the obvious concern about being chained to a radiator for a couple of months with my wife pawning her jewellery to secure my release, it would slow our journey down somewhat. And I didn't like the idea of swapping notes with Terry Waite on the after dinner circuit when we got home. Although I supposed it would add a couple of interesting chapters to the book.

After watching a couple MORE episodes of *The Long Way Round* and again seeing our intrepid heroes take self-defence lessons for their survival in Eastern Europe, we decided we wouldn't be doing the same: first, because I can't fight and second, because I have lost every fight I've ever been in. No, what was needed, I thought, was one of those hand-held electric shock thingamajigs, a sort of mini cattle-prod that gives out about 50,000 volts to any would-be attacker. A friend of mine had somehow gotten one back into the UK and assured me that it had worked to great effect on his neighbour's Alsatian dog. I thought it would be great to own one, if only to clear a path to my Mojito in a crowded pub.

We had studied the map, planned the route and talked over the equipment we would need. If we were going to do this properly we needed to keep diaries, a video diary and film the entire trip. Pete, being the technological whiz-kid, decided that the HD cameras must be Canon and that we needed separate camcorders to work our helmet cams. It turned out we would be carrying more electronic gear than Apollo 11 took to the moon.

It was a long journey home alone in that empty van, but my head was buzzing! The departure date for our trip was getting nearer, arrangements were coming together and I was truly excited about following in the tracks of Che.

Chapter 3
Sun, sea, sand and Che

Che Guevara was the guy with the beard wearing a beret with a star on it whose image appears on T-shirts, badges, bags, and so on. He was Fidel Castro's right-hand man during the Cuban Revolution in the late 1950s and early 1960s.

Although he is famous for being a Cuban citizen, revolutionary leader and freedom fighter, Ernesto 'Che' Guevara was actually Argentinian. Born into a very affluent family in June 1928 in Rosario, Argentina, he made several trips around Latin America in his teens and early twenties, including the one featured in *The Motorcycle Diaries* with his friend Alberto Granado. It was during this trip in 1952 that he saw how the Latin Americans were being oppressed by what he called 'the Yankee friend' (the USA) and the endemic poverty they suffered. He then became involved in political activity. He was what I would describe as a bit of a lad. He was a womaniser, he liked motorcycles and, as it turned out, he liked a fight.

'Che' (which was a popular form of address in Argentina) was a nickname given to him by the Cubans. He became a myth, a legend and an international martyr-figure upon his death in 1967. He was a revolutionary fighter, a military strategist, a medical doctor and a friend and confidante of Fidel Castro.

Ernesto Guevara's dream was to unite Latin America and the rest of the developing world through armed revolution, and to end the poverty, injustice and oppression that he had seen with his own eyes on his travels with Alberto. Che drove himself with fanatical zeal and in the end he paid the ultimate price for his cause. He was captured and executed in Bolivia on 8th October, 1967 on the orders of the American government. His remains, along with those of his companions, were buried in an unmarked grave in a bid to stop him being seen as a martyr. Well that certainly worked didn't it? October 8th is designated the day of the Heroic Guerrilla in Cuba. In 1997 his and the other guerrilla's remains were finally located and returned to Cuba where they were placed in a memorial at Santa Clara, which was the scene of Che Guevara's finest victory during the Cuban Revolution. How the hell were Pete and I supposed to follow that?

You might not believe this but coincidentally my wife Mandie had booked a holiday for us in Cuba. My first thought wasn't about the luxury hotel in Varadero or the all-inclusive Mojitos and Piña coladas I would be consuming, but the fact that Che's friend Alberto Granado was still alive, and I had read somewhere, living in Havana. This was my chance to meet the man who, 56 years previously, had made the same trip we were about to embark upon.

I e-mailed the Cuban Embassy in London explaining about our motorcycle trip and how we were following Che and Alberto, and that it would be an absolute honour to meet this great man.

The Ambassador and his staff must have been very busy at the time as they didn't get back to me right away. In fact, they never got back to me at all! I didn't think I was asking a lot. I'm sure I would have had a lot to talk about with Alberto. Here was a man who had been there, seen it all and got the T-shirt. All I wanted to do was pick his brains on his puncture repair technique and tyre lever manoeuvres on a Norton 500. I checked my e-mail every day but to no avail, perhaps they didn't understand my English.

Pete was busy working on the website for our trip which we had decided to name Revolution Road; it seemed very appropriate as we were following the road that sort of led to the Cuban revolution. We had already shot the beach footage with the Nortons and we decided we needed to introduce ourselves and explain what our trip was about. I decided I would shoot my footage outside the final resting place of our intrepid freedom fighter in Cuba; I had seen the large statue of him on television. I had it pictured in my head: zoom onto the statue of Che, pan away onto me wearing a T-shirt and shorts holding a copy of *The Motorcycle Diaries* and speaking those immortal words, 'Hi, I'm Steve Holmes, here I am at the final resting place, etc, etc.' What could be better?

The Cuban holiday was upon us in no time. The Embassy hadn't replied, but no matter, this was two weeks of total luxury we were embarking on.

On arriving at the hotel we got the customary welcome, the free cocktail and the big sell on the excursions and trips that were available. We booked to swim with dolphins and for the obligatory trip to the capital, Havana, but the trip I was really excited about was the three cities excursion. This took in Santa Clara where Che's mausoleum and final resting place was, Trinidad and finally Cienfuegos (one hundred fires). While the final two cities held no interest for me, I decided that the 15-hour coach trip was worth it just to get the film footage I needed for the website introduction.

We were picked up from our hotel at 5.30 a.m., a ridiculous hour when you're on holiday. The free alcohol from the previous night didn't help, but an inner excitement overcame this as we set off on our journey to the city of the final battle of the revolution. This battle had been led by Che Guevara and had toppled the Fulgencio Batista government in 1958. This victory for the revolutionary troops was seen as the decisive moment in the Cuban Revolution as President Batista fled Cuba less than 12 hours later.

As we approached the Mausoleo Che Guevara we were told we would have a guided tour of the museum dedicated to Guevara's life and a visit to the tomb and final resting place, which houses the remains of Che Guevara and six of his fellow combatants killed in 1967 in Bolivia. It's a resplendent building constructed entirely of concrete. A 100-foot-long wall carries a depiction of the struggle and heroism of the guerrilla fighters. This is overshadowed by a 60-foot plinth on which stands the magnificent bronze statue of Guevara, dressed in full combats with his rifle held at his side. The words on the brass plate read, *Hasta La Victoria Siempre,* 'Forever until Victory'.

The museum gave me a great insight into the man. In his childhood through to his teenage years and his time training to be a doctor his creativity and artistry were to the fore, and then they were replaced by guerrilla combats, medals and firearms. He changed so much in such a short time; but he certainly made his mark on the world.

On entering the mausoleum the first thing I noticed was the cold, but it was clear that it was a very revered place and it was very humbling to be there. On leaving the tomb it was time to capture what we had come for. Mandie was given a quick lesson on how to use the camcorder and then, standing in front of the massive statue, I looked into the camera as she zoomed in on me, 'Hi I'm Steve Holmes,' but the wind took hold of my hastily written script and I totally messed it up. Take two, then three, four – I couldn't get it right. People were watching, wondering what the hell I was doing and we were rapidly running out of the 15 minutes we were allowed to spend at this sacred place before the coach left for the next destination. 'Right this is it,' I called. 'Three, two, one, go.' Mandie pressed the button on the camcorder, gave me the thumbs up and I read the script, which was now stuck to her chest, perfectly. We then ran back to the waiting coach and set off for Parque del Tren Blindado, which is where Che and his forces derailed a train full of back-up tanks, guns and ammunition heading for the government troops, contributing to their defeat.

With the script for the short film now firmly branded in my mind, I decided to do a few more takes at the train crash site. I was getting good at this. I could see myself as a news reporter: 'This is Steve Holmes, Santa Clara, Cuba, for *News at Ten.*' Easy.

When we finally arrived back at the hotel at approximately 10.30 p.m., I swore to myself I would never take a coach excursion again, though what felt like the longest day of my life was worth it for the footage we had taken. It had also been quite a moving day, visiting the mausoleum and final resting place of a young man, whose adventures I was soon to follow.

The rest of my Cuban experience was a mix of fun, laughter and a realisation that socialism just doesn't seem to work. The Cubans are a very friendly bunch, they sell the best cigars, get free power supplies to their homes, have a low crime rate and the lowest illiteracy rate in the Latin world. But they can never own their own homes, and the place is literally falling to bits. With very little investment since the Americans pulled out, the buildings are crumbling and it is a very poor country. The government owns everything. That said, the doctors and nurses are brilliant, as I found out two days before I was due to come home.

Being the finely toned athlete I am I was enticed into a game of beach volleyball by the entertainment staff. As I dived, yes, dived for a return shot I had no chance of getting, I dislocated my right shoulder. It was excruciating! I was close to tears; no I lie, I was in tears.

Entering the medical room of the hotel was like walking onto the set of a *Carry On* film. The nurse's white uniform looked like it had been purchased from an Ann Summers store – apparently Barbara Windsor was about to attend to my dislocated shoulder. I explained what had happened and the nurse gave me two paracetamol tablets before ringing the local hospital.

While I was waiting in the hotel reception for the ambulance to take me to the hospital, the nurse came up to me and gave me an injection in my upper thigh; I was just grateful I was wearing shorts at the time. I felt happier when my wife joined me as she is a qualified nurse and was a great source of help as she laughed at the predicament I was in.

We didn't have to wait long for the ambulance. It was a great big 1950s American car with the name of a *clinico* on the doors, my only surprise was that it wasn't being driven by Marlon Brando. The driver seemed to have the knack of going over every bump and pothole on the roads, each of which gave my arm a sharp jolt, and made the journey seem longer than the coach trip to Las Tres Ciudades two days earlier.

When we arrived at the clinic I was greeted at reception and shown through to the treatment room. I felt like I had stepped back in time. I sat on what can be only described as a slab, a flat steel bed, while I was given gas and air from the glass jars behind me. The last time I had seen jars with rubber bungs was at school in my chemistry lessons. Still the gas was doing its job and the pain was subsiding a little.

The female doctor who attended me resembled my chemistry teacher Mrs Lochhead, and explained to me that I would have to be X-rayed and that the orthopaedic doctor was on his way. The X-ray was taken while the radiographer stood behind an old wooden door. I followed him through to the darkroom where he dipped the film into a series of different chemicals and there was the picture of my shoulder, or at least where it should have been: it was under my armpit somewhere.

I was taken back to the slab when the orthopaedic doctor arrived. He laid me down on the cold metal bed and proceeded to manipulate my shoulder back into place. With a slight click and a whole lot of pain, I was back to normal. As he strapped the arm to my upper torso the other doctor explained to my wife that we could claim the ambulance, X-ray and treatment on our holiday insurance. Holiday insurance! The one thing you should always take out when booking a holiday, is insurance. My wife thought I had arranged the insurance. I thought she had done it. Neither of us had. However, after we had given the doctors an amount of convertible Cuban pesos equivalent to about £100 and explained that we didn't want a receipt, everybody seemed happy. No matter where you go cash is king and as I was to find out later, so are the Cuban doctors.

Cuba was beautiful, the holiday was great and the people fantastic. My only sadness was not meeting Alberto Granado. I was told he had moved back to Buenos Aires a couple of years before, so our liaison would have to wait until we got to Argentina.

On arriving home, the first thing I wanted to do was watch the camcorder footage we had shot for the website on our marathon trip to Santa Clara. As I sat back in the armchair and pressed play on the camcorder, all I could see on the TV screen were pictures of my wife's feet and legs and a howling wind. Five times this happened. I was horrified. Apparently when she thought she'd been turning the camcorder on, she'd been turning it off and vice versa. Still, the film we had shot at the train crash site looked great. I looked a real hunk of beefcake stood there in my Che Guevara T-shirt, brandishing my copy of *The Motorcycle Diaries*, with the train carriages from the battle of Santa Clara in the background. But the words coming out of my mouth were drowned out by the howling wind and the sound of car horns. The 15-hour coach journey we had endured to shoot the film had been to no avail, as the film was terrible, not even a decent 'Hi, I'm Steve Holmes.'

I spent the next couple of weeks exchanging e-mails with Pete and slowly purchasing the spares, helmet and clothing I would need. I saw an old leather flying helmet for sale on eBay and thought it might look good in some of the photos we would be taking, a sort of 1950s' motorcyclist/fighter pilot look. As I was going out that evening I asked my sister Lisa if she would bid on the leather hat for me, it was currently at £16 with a couple of hours to go. I told her my maximum bid was £25. When I arrived home that evening I was greeted by the good news that I had won the bidding for the leather helmet – against my wife! She had spotted that I was watching the item and had proceeded to start a bidding war, unbeknown to her, against my sister. Between them they had managed to drive the price up from £16 to £28.

I received the helmet in record time and wrote to the seller to tell him I would cherish it and where it was about to go, I received a lovely reply from a gentleman named Herbert Miller Crook:

Steve, Thanks for your e-mail and the link! Most interesting. I can only wish you both, very good luck during your epic journey. To think where the old helmet is to go!! Unable to accompany you, I am approaching my 83rd birthday. The helmet was worn by my late father on his belt driven Toredor?

I think. Later on his Royal Enfield, during the 1920s. As a young boy of 7 years I wore the helmet as pillion passenger on the back of Dad's bike – memories! Regards to you both, Bert

I was really touched when I receive this e-mail, not only because of the history behind the helmet, but because I realised the memories behind that history.

Mid-September and it was time to travel down to Hayling Island again. This time we were going to a place called Netley Marsh, which is just outside Southampton, to a Euro jumble which is basically a massive car boot sale for old bike fanatics. That isn't how I saw it though. As we meandered round the vast array of stalls it looked to me like somebody had dredged the *Titanic* from the seabed and put the different pieces on sale. I had never seen so much junk in all my life. As we stood by one stall I thought that if somebody had left this pile of crap by my house I would phone the council. At that point someone came along and managed to barter the stallholder down to £60 for the lot. Hey, what do I know about genuine British bike parts?

Eventually, I was £180 lighter and carrying tyres, motorcycle chains, batteries, tyre levers and many electrical parts back to Pete's car. Yes a fool and his money are lucky to be together in the first place. I had got caught up in the fervour of this Mecca of motorcycle parts and had duly treated the Norton to a few spares. It was the first time I had witnessed for myself that age-old saying 'one man's junk is another man's treasure'. As we were leaving Netley Marsh, one guy was wheeling what I can only describe as the keel of the 1912 White Star liner on a trolley, back to his car, thinking he had purchased a bargain.

Over the next couple of months, I acquired most of the things I needed for the trip: motorcycle boots, open face helmet, leather trousers and a water purifier. In fact everything I needed to be a real rocker.

My one phobia in life is needles. Not the knitting or sewing variety, but the ones administered by doctors and nurses. I hate injections. For this trip I needed yellow fever, typhoid, hepatitis B, tetanus, in fact everything except bubonic plague. What ever happened to administering drugs via sugar cubes? To add insult to injury I had to pay for the pleasure of having somebody stick needles into me. Over the course of the next few weeks I attended the clinic and was ever so brave while the nurse stuck the giant needles into me.

The weeks were passing by quickly now, we had booked our flights, sorted out the shipping of the bikes to Argentina and everything seemed to be falling into place. Except which bike I would be riding!

Pete had tried to sort out the 1937 Norton, but hadn't had time to work on it. The engine out of the 1950 Norton which we knew to be okay, wouldn't fit into the frame of the 16H, so it was a case of switching the forks from one bike to the other, to give it that authentic Che Guevara Norton look. KOP 27 was going to Argentina.

'Steve Patterson's the name,' the guy at James Cargo told us as we entered the workshop to have the bikes gift wrapped, for their long journey via cargo ship to Buenos Aires. I sat on the Norton as it was strapped down onto a pallet that had brought a brand new BMW motorcycle into England. Steve put the cardboard wrap around the Norton and then sealed the lid. It was like the bike had been put into a coffin as he put the last screw into the giant box. The next time I would see the bike would be when we were reunited in South America in a month's time. As a last gesture I scrubbed out the words BMW Motorad, Germany, which were printed onto the side of the box. I wrote on instead, Norton, England. Steve laughed, he thought we were crazy to be attempting an 8,000 mile trip on these old timers.

Chapter 4
An open and shut case

When a man hits 40, he seems to rebel, as if to show the world that he is still young enough to pull a girl younger than himself. He is, after all, a primate. Deep down the insecurities of getting old are setting in. He grows his hair (if he still has any), gets his ear pierced, gets a tattoo (probably tribal) and buys a motorcycle. Go to any meeting where motorcyclists gather and 98 per cent of them will be over 40 years old, the born-again biker. An adventurer who has discovered the freedom that speed on two wheels brings. Those often uttered words, 'he's going through a midlife crisis,' apply to many crusaders of the road, but not to me.

I am 50 years old and how many people do you know who live to be 100? I am past the midlife stage, so for me this adventure is a well thought out thing and not an impulsive midlife decision. Although I would still like to be a train driver when I grow up.

The cold bit my face on that freezing January morning as I walked along Hayling Island's shale beach with my wife. We were scheduled to leave Heathrow at 6.50 p.m. and I spent the last few hours throwing pebbles into the Channel and discussing, believe it or not, my funeral arrangements. For the music I had decided on Charles Villiers Stanford's *Beati Quorum* to be sung by Blackburn Cathedral choir and I didn't want the curtains to be closed at the cremation. The things that you think about when leaving a loved one for three months seem almost surreal. Your plans for the future all talked about, but also the realisation that an 8,000 mile motorcycle trip on foreign shores brings with it a host of dangers.

All the plans over the last few months had come to fruition and this was the day we would part, for at least two and a half months. We both shed a few tears on the beach: mine due to the cold and Mandie's to a mis-thrown pebble of mine. Aimed at the Solent it had hit her on the back of the head.

I had borrowed two old suitcases for the trip, which I intended to throw away when I had loaded the stuff onto the bike. One was a bright pink case which no one was likely to steal; the other was a suitcase that the late Provost of Blackburn Cathedral had carried his cassocks in. It was given to me by his daughter. In one I packed my clothes and bare essentials for riding the bike and in the other my tent, sleeping bag, and so on.

Walking back from the beach, reality kicked in. This was it: we would soon be on our way. We would soon be following Che Guevara and Alberto Granado's path, but to me this was *our* adventure.

The drive to Heathrow seemed to go quickly. We parked the car, grabbed a couple of trolleys and headed towards the Iberia check-in desk. I said my goodbyes to my wife and the tears rolled for real this time.

The flight was in a couple of hours but there were only the two of us standing at the desk. We were due to fly to Buenos Aires with a change at Madrid's Barajas airport. We soon found out why we were the only people queuing. Madrid airport was closed due to snow and it could take up to three days before it would be clear. Snow, Madrid, they shouldn't be in the same sentence. I couldn't believe it. What a start! I just hoped this wasn't how things would continue.

The Rafa Benitez look-alike at the Iberia information desk told us that he would be able to guarantee us a flight in 24 hours. My wife was already halfway up the M6, so it looked like we would be spending the first night at the airport. There was one alternative. We could go on standby for a British Airways flight that left at 8.35 p.m. that evening. If two people didn't turn up for the flight, we would be able to go that evening.

We decided to chance it and got the shuttle to the infamous terminal 5, the Bermuda triangle of terminals which has lost more cases than the Crown Prosecution Service. We were stunned by how many people were on standby with us, all hoping that they didn't have to spend the night on the cold, hard airport floor. The BA staff were very helpful and friendly, but they didn't hold out much hope of us getting on flight 247 to Buenos Aires via Sao Paulo, Brazil.

We had over two hours to kill before they announced which lucky contestants had got through the lottery of who would get on the flight. I bought a tuna sandwich and a can of Red Bull which came to about the same price as the budget deficit of Libya. The minutes ticked by slowly. A family we had spoken to had got the last five seats on the British Airways flight and a sixth member of their party had the chance to go on standby with us. They couldn't risk it as they were due to meet a ship to go on the cruise of a lifetime round the Antarctic. They opted to pay £6,000 pounds for a first class seat instead. That was considerably more than I had paid for my tuna sandwich and can of Red Bull and it gave us very little hope of getting on the flight. I mean who doesn't turn up for their flight?

Well a couple of idiots obviously didn't, because at 8.25 p.m. the names of Holmes and Sandford were called at the standby gate. We were cock-a-hoop. The feeling of elation was unbelievable; we had literally won the lottery. I couldn't stop smiling, we sprinted to gate 48B, showed

our boarding cards and got on board flight 247 to Buenos
Aires. We were on our way and would arrive earlier than
if we had taken the flight via Madrid.

The family who had taken the upgrade were seated
near us and congratulated us on getting the flight. The
sixth member of their party, who was in first class,
kept peeking through the curtain and teasing them
as she polished off glass after glass of complimentary
champagne. Who could blame her? For the price of that
ticket, I would have wanted shares in the vineyard.

On Saturday 10th January, 2009 we landed in Buenos
Aires where we had made prior arrangements to stay
with a couch-surfing host.

Couch-surfing is a website/network via which people
from all over the world offer accommodation to travellers
and backpackers. Basically a spare couch or bed they let
free of charge to fellow globetrotters. You can return the
favour should people decide to visit your town.

Our host was a fellow motorcyclist who had offered
us a place to stay on our first night in Buenos Aires. His
webpage profile read well: a friendly guy, who would
show you the sights and scenery of Buenos Aires. In his
picture he was dressed in black, seated on a motorcycle
and wearing sunglasses over which sprouted a thick
black mono-brow. To complement the mono-brow he
had a thick mop of black curly hair, a big black bushy
beard and a menacing smile. He looked to me like an
expert in wielding an axe, a machete, indeed anything
that could disembowel a human being. To all intents
and purposes, our host to be looked like a stereotypical
mass murderer! When he didn't show up to meet us, I
was more than a little relieved, although it did mean we
would have to find alternative accommodation.

We decided to stop at a place called Dakar Motos,
which is in the Florida district, in the north of Buenos

Aires. This was where the people who were to arrange the bikes' clearance through customs and all the paperwork and insurance had an office. Dakar Motos has a workshop, a camping area and a few beds at which fellow travelling motorcyclists pitch up and rest, drink and swap tips and tales of their travels through South America. All we had to do was find it.

We walked out of the airport into the kiln-like heat and decided to get a taxi. We hadn't a clue where we were going, had been travelling for two days and just needed a base where we could take a shower and sort out our arrangements. The air was filled with diesel fumes mixed with a smell of caramel and perspiration. The loudly blasting car horns sounded like the London Philharmonic Orchestra warming up for a sonata. It was vibrant. We were surrounded by cab drivers, eager for our newly acquired pesos. We must have looked like American tourists, especially with my bright pink suitcase. We negotiated a rate of $120 (Argentinian pesos) and as the cab driver loaded the car with our luggage we were relieved to have got away from the airport and on our way.

We arrived at the street in the backwater district of Buenos Aires where Dakar Motos was supposed to be. We were dropped off, but there was no sign of the place. Down the road two motorcyclists were loaded up on BMW 1200 GS bikes and looked to be heading on their way. We flagged them down to ask them where Dakar Motos was. They told us to knock at two steel doors that were further down the road. The cab driver left us with his pocket bulging full of pesos, probably the equivalent of a week's wages. Yes, we had been legally mugged – £25 for the 20-minute ride.

We faced the two grey steel doors, surely this couldn't be it? We knocked and the doors were opened by Brian, a Canadian who had been on the road for nine months with his girlfriend Marie. We entered Dakar Motos.

At the front is the garage and workshop where Javier, the owner, stores and repairs motorcycles. Unfortunately he was out of town as he was following the Dakar rally, which was being held in South America that year. His partner and co-owner, Sandra, wouldn't be around until tomorrow.

We were shown through to the living quarters, which consisted of four bunk beds, a sink, table, cooker and a fridge that had more green fur in it than Epping Forest. My heart sank; it was an absolute shit-tip. I have seen better mattresses being thrown onto bonfires to celebrate the demise of Guy Fawkes on November the fifth. I couldn't possibly spend the night there. Pete unpacked his computer and quickly arranged for us to spend the following two nights at a couch-surfer's place in the San Telmo district of Buenos Aires. But for our first night we had no choice, we would have to stay at Dakar.

I unpacked my toiletries and threw my sleeping bag on the top bunk; I then took a cold shower and changed my clothes. Hunger pangs ripped through my stomach. I was starving. A visit to a local supermarket, where I purchased bread, liquid bread (aka Stella Artois) and chicken, which I cooked on the barbecue, satisfied my appetite. We then walked to the local train station where we caught a train to the centre of Buenos Aires for about 30 pence. We had a walk round the centre and then headed back to the Mecca that is Dakar Motos. A couple more Stellas and then I climbed into the flea-pit that was to be my bed for the night. Exhausted, weary and drained I slept like a baby.

Sandra, who was sorting the customs clearance for the Nortons was due to meet up with us to explain what paperwork we would need, how much it would cost us and, most importantly, how long it would take us to get the bikes through customs. I was busy counting the mosquito bites on my legs when she walked in.

Sandra smiled warmly as she kissed each of us on both cheeks, and offered us coffee. She had long flowing chestnut hair and Latin fire burning in her smouldering brown eyes. She was a sprightly woman, slim, tall and dynamic, and she smoked like a second-hand Lada. She explained to us that the customs office had just returned to work after the Christmas holiday and that they had a backlog of things to deal with. The customs clearance could take up to a week. A whole week would be one hell of a setback but we were optimistic it wouldn't take that long – Sandra had just helped out a guy from New Zealand who had struggled to get his bike into Argentina by himself and had sorted out his customs problems in one day.

Javier, her partner was a big gangly guy. Proprietor and mechanic at Dakar Motos, he had a short crop of red hair and looked like an extra from *Braveheart*. His gravelly voice sounded like he had been singing karaoke all night and he too smoked heavily. A keen motorcyclist, he spent his time between the workshop repairing bikes and riding with his friends Carlos and Fabrizio who were two tall, slim guys. In fact everybody in South America seemed to be slim which gave me some reassurance about our time in Colombia, as fat people are harder to kidnap.

We took the train to Retiro station in Buenos Aires and walked to San Telmo which is the oldest *barrio* (neighbourhood) in the city. It is characterised by colonial buildings, cafés, tango parlours and antique shops which line the cobblestoned streets. Filled with artists and dancers, the main square, Plaza Dorrego, hosts a semi-permanent antique fair and tango-related activities for both locals and tourists and has a real Bohemian feel to it.

Our couch-surfing hosts lived in this vibrant district and as we rang the bell, I was a little apprehensive. It seemed really strange to me that people would let total strangers from around the world into their homes. Perhaps I had watched too many Hammer House of Horror films, but this would be a perfect scenario for a mass murderer to woo in victims. We were greeted at the door by Alejandro, another slim Latin American who had short-cropped hair and a warm smile. I was immediately put at my ease as he introduced us to his wife, Mariana, and suggested that as we were British we may want to go to the pub. Alejandro was a big football fan and liked a pint or two so we had a lot in common. He seemed to like a lot of British culture, especially the Beatles, Manchester United and real ale.

When we got back to their apartment we were shown our bed for the evening, a double bed settee. We were instructed that there was a no nudity rule in the house and then they both retired to their room. Pete and I got ready for bed, and fully obeying the no nudity rule, climbed into bed partly dressed.

The following morning, we decided to explore the city. Buenos Aires (which translates as fair winds or good air) is a city of some 13 million people.

We visited all the usual sight-seeing places: the Plaza de Mayo, Plaza San Martin, the cathedral. We had a lot of time on our hands and took the underground train, which saved me walking in my flip-flops. The trains were packed and at one stop a rather stunning girl got on the train and smiled at me. I wondered why the hell she was smiling at an old bugger like me, and then I felt the zips on my shorts being unzipped. No, it's not what you are thinking – it was her accomplice going through my pockets searching for my wallet. A gang of pickpockets was on the train and she was the decoy. It happened so quickly that before I had fully realised what was going on they had got off the train. Fortunately for me my wallet was intact and all my documents were safe in my back pocket.

A phone call from Sandra that night gave us the bad news that the bikes were going to take longer than first thought due to red tape with the customs and a glitch with the shipping documents. We were going to have to wait until Friday, at the earliest, before we could pick the bikes up.

Our hosts Alejandro and Mariana offered us a third night at their place. They are two wonderful people who epitomise the warmth and hospitality that I found during the rest of our journey among the Argentinian people. I was grateful that we didn't have to return to Dakar Motos and the infestation of mosquitoes there.

We spent the next day exploring the city, pounding the streets. My flip-flops were killing me and my feet were pretty cut up. I began staring at people's shoes wondering how comfortable they were. I was like some sexual deviant with a foot fetish. I hoped we would find a mosque in this mostly Catholic country, just so I could switch shoes with somebody who had left their shoes at the entrance while they were praying. That night we again enjoyed the finest Argentinian hospitality, sharing *empanadas* washed down with a few bottles of Quilmes.

We had to leave Alejandro and Mariana's apartment the next day. We said goodbye on the Plaza de Mayo and went our separate ways. Once again we caught the underground train, this time to the upmarket district of Palermo. This is where the Guevara family home was, where Che and Alberto said goodbye to Che's parents. This was where they started their motorcycle trip from, so this is where we'd start our trip too. The address? 2180, Calle Araoz, Palermo, Buenos Aires.

The original Guevara family home had been razed to the ground many years before and replaced by a block of apartments. Passing locals watching us photographing the modern building told us, 'Che Guevara used to live here.' Whatever you think of Che Guevara, the Argentinians speak his name with pride. There was no plaque on the modern building, but everything surrounding it was exactly the same as it was when they had set off on their Norton all those years ago. All we needed now was our Nortons.

We had no alternative but to pitch up back at Dakar Motos that night. It was where we would be sleeping until we got our bikes through customs. Over the course of the next few days we visited the customs department to pay for insurance, photocopies, clearance and storage. Then it was import duty and tax. We spent the majority of our time catching the train from Florida in the north of the city to Retiro in the centre. In-between all the form-filling and parting with cash we did a hell of a lot of sight-seeing! Recoleta cemetery, where Eva Peron and the wealthy of Buenos Aires are buried, is an amazing place. The tombs are unbelievable and ghoulish as it seems, it is both a fascinating and beautiful place to visit.

On the Sunday morning Fabrizio, a friend of Javier from Dakar Motos, took us for early morning breakfast by the Río de la Plata. The scenery was stunning and that day, after what I had seen over the last couple of days, I fell in love with Buenos Aires.

We headed for the Boca area of Buenes Aires, and a street called La Caminito. This is the old port district, famous for its football team, La Boca Juniors. The buildings were painted in a mix of colours, lime greens with reds, purples with orange, whatever the mixture, it was a dis-chord to the eye but absolute harmony to the mind. Latino music filled the air and tango dancers strutted the streets like proud peacocks. We sat there for most of the day watching the array of people pass us by. There was a carnival atmosphere, a crescendo of noise, a Mexican wave of South American culture. La Caminito was a place of wonder and beauty that I will never forget.

That night we received a phone call from Sandra, we were to meet her at Retiro station at 8.30 a.m. the following day, bringing with us our passports, our helmets and anything else we needed to ride the bikes. We were cautiously elated, but we had been let down too many times over the last ten days to be sure this was it.

We were up early and arrived at Retiro at 7.40 a.m. We grabbed a coffee beside the station and saw the flip-side of Buenos Aires: seven young boys all huddled together under a blanket sleeping rough on the streets. It broke my heart to see that type of thing in a major city in this day and age.

Sandra arrived at 8.30 prompt. Over the last couple of days I had been thinking about how good she would look in something long and flowing, like the Río de la Plata. I'd been repeatedly let down, and here she was again, looking officious in smart jacket, jeans and boots. Sandra told us there was a good chance we would get our bikes that day. We headed for the release house where we needed to get a signature from the head of customs. Two hours later, with the signature safely in Sandra's portfolio, we got a taxi to the docks. I was becoming very optimistic. Six hours later, after an eternity of form-filling and customs lunch breaks, we were lead through to the warehouse, where a box with the words, 'Norton, England' written in felt tip pen stood before me. I couldn't stop smiling. Pete couldn't stop smiling, even Sandra couldn't stop smiling. Here were the Nortons!

After a frame and engine number check by a customs officer, we wheeled the bikes out into the 38 degree heat. It was the first time these two old machines had ventured onto foreign soil. Pete kicked his bike, nothing. Second kick, a cough and plume of black smoke and she was running. I kicked mine, nothing. Again, nothing. 'C'mon girl,' I thought, and then she took her first breath of Argentine air and burst into life. The hairs on my neck stood up and I had a smile on my face wider than the Río de la Plata. Sandra couldn't believe it and burst out laughing. The crowd of customs officers and warehouse workers that had gathered smiled in bewilderment. Heads shaking, they couldn't believe the journey we would soon be undertaking. I put my open face helmet on, selected first gear and rode her to the dock gate. I handed over the release form to the security guard, the barrier lifted and before me was the open road. Remember, the furthest I had been on this bike, was about two miles back in England. I was like an excited schoolboy fumbling at a bra strap for the first time; I didn't know what I was doing, but I got there in the end.

It was about five miles to Dakar Motos and this would be the first true test for me and the 59-year-old machine. We set off in the direction of Florida and our home for the last few days, Dakar Motos. We did our best to avoid the potholes in the roads that should have had 'mining subsidence' warnings next to them. The looks we got as we rode our bikes through the busy streets were amazing. When we stopped at traffic lights we were almost mobbed, drivers from the cars on either side of us asked: What is it? How many cc's? How fast? How old?

The Argentinians loved those bikes and so did I. I might as well have been riding Kate Moss, the supermodel. The attention she was attracting was unbelievable. I felt like I had a new girlfriend, and she didn't just turn heads, she broke necks! Everybody wanted a piece of her, she was different, she was unique, and she was mine.

As we pulled up at Dakar Motos, the street seemed to be filled with people holding cameras and taking photographs. It is a haven for motorcycle travellers through South America, but nobody had attempted the journey on two old machines like these. I was just pleased she had made it the five miles from the port to Dakar through very heavy traffic. Only 8,000 more miles to go.

We would be setting off early in the morning, so we had to load the bikes up and get them ready for the journey ahead. This was easier said than done. My panniers were already full, holding a camping stove, tools, inner tubes, spare chains and cables. I added my clothes to that lot and the panniers were full to bursting. The contents of the bright pink case were all on the bike, either in my rucksack or in the panniers. There was nothing else for it – the Provost's old cassock suitcase would have to make the journey with me. My sleeping mat, sleeping bag and tent fitted in perfectly, it seemed made for the job, so I strapped it tightly on to the back of the Norton.

I didn't sleep properly that night, I don't know if it was apprehension, excitement or the fact that I hadn't had a couple of beers. Pete and I had looked at his collection of 1950s Esso road maps and studied the routes. I felt like a drunk who had been hit over the head by a press-gang and woken up in Buenos Aires. This was it, the start of our epic journey. I looked across at my Norton; she was loaded up like the old jalopy out of *The Beverley Hillbillies* but to me she was beautiful, she was *Kate*, the supermodel.

Chapter 5
La aventura comienza

'If it's not leaking oil, then there isn't any in it,' was the reply I once got when I asked an elderly Norton rider why his bike was losing so much oil. British motorcycles are renowned for oil leaks, and on the morning of Tuesday, 20th January I realised that *Kate* had taken it to the extreme. Looking at the puddle of oil on the floor of Dakar Motos I figured they would have a bigger clean-up operation than the Alaskan Government had when the Exxon Valdez spilled her load into Prince William Sound. This was something I would have to keep an eye on. Pete's bike had only a few spots of oil under her whereas *Kate* was bleeding the black stuff profusely.

This was the day we had been waiting for, all the planning and hard work that had been taking place over the last few months was to be put to the test. We would be leaving what had been our home for the last ten days, our Buenos Aires comfort zone, and setting off on our adventure.

A crowd of fellow motorcyclists gathered outside Dakar Motos: a Texan named Chuck, who had befriended us during our stay, Carlos and Fabrizio and a few other adventurers who were staying at Dakar.

As we were geeing ourselves up to start our journey, we heard the familiar sound of a Norton 500 coming towards us. It pulled up outside Dakar, next to our bikes and glistened in the bright Buenos Aires sunshine. It was a real minter but what was an old Norton doing here?

It was owned by an Argentinian gentleman by the name of Gustavo Agra, a sprightly man who had the look of a white haired Rolf Harris, his beaming smile lit up his face as he looked at the three Nortons parked side-by-side. He had built and restored the Norton motorcycles for *The Motorcycle Diaries* and he was riding the actual bike that had starred in the movie. He had heard we would be attempting the route featured in Che Guevara's diary and was very interested in how two Englishmen had shipped two of these classic motorcycles to his homeland, to emulate the epic journey.

Gustavo's Norton was a masterpiece that had been restored to perfection. Every piece of chromework gleamed in the sunlight, every nut and bolt had been replaced and there was not a drop of oil in sight. His motorcycle looked like it had just rolled off the production line from James Lansdowne Norton's motorcycle factory in Birmingham.

Sandwiched between Gustavo's and Pete's pristine machines was my Norton, the unrestored waif of this Norton family. However, she was the one attracting the most attention from Gustavo. All the paint was original and he got his slide gauge out to measure the pinstripe lines on the tank. The man was a perfectionist where Nortons were concerned and he wanted to make sure he had built his own to the exact standards the Norton factory had stipulated. He poured over the bikes like he was the quality control inspector at the original factory and nodded approvingly. *Kate* had a real originality about her and in my eyes she was a rose between two thorns, the Cinderella with her two ugly sisters. We chatted about the route we would be taking, the oil we would be using and lots of other technical jargon I didn't understand, but thankfully Pete did! We took lots of photographs of each other's bikes and then there were handshakes and hugs all round and it was time for us to go. I put my 'pisspot' open-faced helmet on and cocked my leg over the Norton. Pete's bike started on the first kick. 'Please start *Kate*,' I thought, as my right foot rested on the kick-start. Everybody was watching, smiling and waving and I didn't want to be embarrassed in front of Gustavo or the watching crowd. First kick, nothing, 'Please, please, please don't let me down,' my foot connected with the kick-start again and pushed down hard, she fired and the Norton engine thumped away like Mohammed Ali in his heyday. I pulled in the clutch, selected first gear and we were on our way, heading towards the Palermo district of downtown Buenos Aires.

We had studied maps and pounded the streets of Buenos Aires for ten days and as we joined the traffic to head towards Avenue Libertador and Che's family home, we knew we were heading in the right direction. It was mayhem as we weaved in and out of traffic on the three lane highway heading downtown: the noise of revving engines, the tooting and growling of a thousand car horns and traffic coming from all directions. Added to the cars, was an endless parade of buses jockeying for position, cutting each other, and us, up. The thick black smoke belching out of their exhausts convinced me that they had found a way of running those vast people transporters on coal!

We found our way to 2180 Araoz, with a little luck and a sense of direction that a homing pigeon would have been proud of. Our wandering round the streets of Buenos Aires had made everything familiar and there we were at the site of the old Guevara family home, about to leave on a trip no one had attempted since 1952. After a lot of photographs to mark the start of our journey, we were seen off, to a round of applause from curious passers-by who had gathered, wondering what two old bikes were doing in the upmarket district of their capital city.

The Nortons soon left the crowds of admirers behind, as we headed towards the *autopista* and the road out of the beautiful city that had briefly been our home. It was late afternoon and we hadn't heeded the advice we had been given to set off early and park up early.

The sun was shining fiercely above us as we hit the slip road and climbed up onto the *autopista*, heading south towards the Atlantic Ocean. I stretched the Norton's legs and climbed to speeds of up to 45 mph! The roads were very poorly maintained and the bike's lack of suspension made every pothole a short sharp shock through my entire body. We were soon leaving behind the built-up city suburbs, and pampas replaced the housing and noise of the capital. Gauchos on horseback herding cattle became a familiar site as we came to the parched, drought-hit flatlands of Argentina. Then it was black burnt-out fields, which went on for miles, evidence of the searing hot summer and the lack of rain they had suffered. Overtaking a truck, a change of road surface catapulted the Norton into the air and, as the unstable motorcycle touched terra firma, she nearly threw me off. It was a leap Eddie Kidd would have been proud of and I slowed up a little. It was *Kate's* way of telling me to respect her: after all, she was carrying a luggage weight equivalent to two passengers, plus me. She certainly wasn't built to perform at high speeds, especially on roads like these.

The most noticeable thing on these open roads was the size of the road kill. Not just the odd flattened rabbit like in England: whatever animals these were would have to be dragged to the side of the road. To be honest, I didn't slow down to examine the victims.

We were a couple of hours into our journey when we were stopped by two roadside police officers. They looked a little bemused and went over the bikes, explaining to us that it was a legal requirement to have your headlight on 24/7 in Argentina. Duly obliging wasn't good enough though, as they then demanded our passports and papers. In true American movie style we got 'good cop, bad cop' and fortunately for me I had the good cop. He checked my papers then admired the old girl beneath me. Unfortunately, Pete wasn't having such a smooth ride with his officer who had obviously watched too many Dirty Harry films and was looking for a promotion from his roadside duties. He scrupulously studied Pete's passport, 'English?' he enquired. Step up the international language of football! It wasn't long before we were having a deep conversation about my beloved Manchester United, Carlos Tevez and indeed *la mano de Dios* (the infamous hand ball by Maradona against England in 1986). A little bit of banter between two old foes and the vigilant officers allowed us on our way.

Another 120 miles into our journey we were flagged down again by a single roadside cop who resembled Mr Bean. 'No headlight, $50 fine,' he explained, checking our papers. I took my papers back off him, told him we didn't understand him and we weren't about to pay any fine. Looking confused, he watched as we climbed back onto our bikes and carried on with our journey.

The fact that my headlight wasn't working was becoming a hindrance to us. It was 10 p.m., the sun was beginning to dip towards the horizon and we were miles from anywhere, surrounded by flat pampas land with not a tree in sight. We were sleepy and suffering from fatigue and needed to find somewhere to spend the night. In the last few minutes of daylight we spotted a clump of eucalyptus trees ahead. Pete had the same thought as me, and in a move Steve McQueen would have been impressed by, we both off-roaded the Nortons down the sheer grass embankment and into the shelter of the trees. Within minutes we had unfurled our sleeping bags, climbed into them fully-clothed and exhausted, and fallen asleep to the mating call of thousands of crickets.

The early morning alarm call of two bright green parrots squawking away like a couple of demented daleks in the eucalyptus trees brought us round. I hadn't envisaged spending my first night sleeping rough in a field next to my Norton, but it was the first time in a while I hadn't been bitten by mosquitoes. We shared a breakfast of water and three biscuits each with the background noise of the parrots mixing with the sounds of a couple of gauchos herding their cattle for an early morning milking session. Pete then had a look at my headlight. The battery wasn't charging so I had no power; this in a country that demanded by law that you keep your headlight on 24 hours a day. Still it could be worse – it could be raining.

Feeling as rough as a robber's dog, I packed my things together and we 'McQueened' back up the sharp embankment and onto the road, heading for Villa Gesell. Within a mile we hit a 24-hour petrol station with camping and showering facilities! I couldn't believe it. We had slept rough, five minutes from an oasis. It was also there that I discovered my first grey pubic hair. Unfortunately for me it was stuck in the pastry I had ordered in the garage restaurant!

After the food and fuel stop we pressed on towards Villa Gesell, 236 miles from Buenos Aires and the first stop Che mentions in his diary. The heat was almost unbearable, it was approaching midday and the temperature was around 36 degrees. The landscape changed from the black fields (evidence of grass fires) into mile upon mile of bright yellow sunflowers, which filled huge fields and seemed to smile at us as we passed by them.

Villa Gesell was a beautiful Atlantic coast resort, a sort of South American Scarborough, very 1930s with a great family bucket and spade atmosphere. It was the place Alberto Granado had first seen the ocean. We rode towards the beach and the road suddenly turned to sand, which made riding those fully laden motorcycles very difficult. My back wheel snaked and slipped under me a couple of times but fortunately, as the centre of gravity was so low, I managed to keep the bike upright and we made it to the beach and witnessed the same sight that greeted Che and Alberto all those years ago. We sat for a few moments and watched the Atlantic waves roll onto the sun-kissed sands that hadn't seen rain for over three months. We relished the moment and then decided to go into town for some food and drink. Kitted up in my helmet and motorcycle gear I kicked and kicked *Kate* until I was exhausted by the heat. I was kicking more than Johnny Wilkinson at Twickenham but still she wouldn't start. Pete had a go but she point-blank refused to start, so there was no alternative but to tow her into town. We attached a strap between Pete's bike and mine and he towed me down the sandy path. When the path became firm enough, I knocked her into gear and bump-started her. Luckily she fired up at the first attempt and *Kate* was smiling again.

Lunch in Villa Gesell was dry bread, cheese and nectarines, washed down with water. We ate at the roadside in the shade of a restaurant awning. Parked on the main road, it wasn't long before the bikes were surrounded by the chefs and staff from the surrounding restaurants and passing holidaymakers. Centre of attention again, *Kate* was revelling in the adulation. It was like a *Vogue* fashion shoot done on camera phones. Everybody wanted to be photographed with her. The break had done her good and after cooling down she fired up on the first kick. Our next port of call would be Miramar, which was further along the coast. The roads were getting a lot rougher and with the lack of suspension, the heat and the dust, riding was beginning to take its toll on me, especially my butt!

We rode along the coast road through Mar Azul, then Mar del Plata, a huge beach resort, which has over 7 million visitors a year. This city is Argentina's largest seaside resort and looked a great place to stay. Che and Alberto just passed right through and that's exactly what we did. It was far too early in the day for us to stop and besides we had sort of budgeted for about 200 miles a day, so we went on to Miramar. Che and Alberto spent a whole week at this resort, but we just stopped for coffee. My bike had to be towed to start it again and for the first time I had doubts creep into my head about *Kate* making the whole trip. The roads were turning into dust and the heat was unbearable and stole my breath away. I was dehydrated, sweating like an Aussie bin man, it was physically and mentally demanding, and we were only on our second day. The highlight of the mundane roads was passing a coach that had gone grass tracking. There was a cow stuck underneath it with pools of blood everywhere and a little further down the road we had to swerve to avoid its leg. The bovine was barbecued by the coach, which had made a right mess of the poor beast.

Necochea was the next town on our route. It lacked the woodsy allure of the resort of Villa Gesell, but was a much bigger coastal town with a port and high rises. We hadn't intended to stay in Necochea but it was getting late, I was sunburnt, I stank and needed a shower, and my underpants had become my best friend. The first hostel I stopped at looked me up and down disapprovingly and gave me the immortal words first thrown at Joseph and Mary 2,000 years ago: 'There is no room at the inn.'

I knew what they really meant: I looked like I was there to start up a branch of Necochea Satan's Slaves. I smelt like a Hell's Angel who had bitten off a chicken's head and pissed on his own jeans. We rode to somewhere a little more downmarket. It was nearer to the beach, it had safe parking for the bikes and a room that resembled the one in which Norman Bates had used a Bowie knife to such great effect. It had a toilet plus cold and cold running water. And a shower curtain that looked like it was covered in blood, but on closer inspection I found to be brown body scale, which I think I probably added to.

Showered, clean-shaven and with my initiation jeans washed, I went from Hell's Angel to Mod and we went out for pizza and a couple of beers. We had an early start in the morning, so I had no intention of drinking on an empty stomach. Giselle, our waitress told us to help ourselves to cold beer from the fridge and she would bring us our pizzas. I liked this town a lot.

We had done two hard days riding, *Kate* had been towed twice, ten no starts, but she had done amazingly well. As I climbed into bed that night, I noticed a huge spider come out of my rucksack and make its way to the bathroom. It had probably hitched a lift the night we had slept in the woods and I wondered if it liked Necochea as much as we did.

We left Necochea the following morning at about 10.30 a.m. The forecast was for the temperature to reach 40 degrees Celsius and it didn't disappoint. The roads obviously hadn't been maintained since Che and Alberto had ridden down them on their Norton all those years ago, and with crosswinds of between 60 and 70 mph it was how I imagined riding with the Devil breathing into your face would be. We rode the girls very hard that day as we headed inland for Bahia Blanca and probably hit speeds of up to 60 mph. The road took us away from the Atlantic through Orense, a picturesque town, then onto the main highway near Coronel Dorrego. The crosswinds were whipping up mini-twisters out of the dust across the pampas. It was sheer hard graft riding in those conditions and we only stopped to refuel and oil up the bikes and to take on food and water ourselves. We rode the whole 210 miles without a break and it took its toll on us: we were exhausted, saddle sore and in need of refreshment.

On arriving in Bahia Blanca we stopped to refuel and buy some more oil at a service station. I think with the amount of oil my bike was using, it had probably pushed up the world price of a barrel by a couple of dollars. On the forecourt we were immediately approached by an Argentinian film crew, from Canal Siete (Channel 7). They were from the news team and after interviewing me and Pete, the supermodels then hogged the limelight as the news crew spent a few minutes filming them. We stopped a couple of miles down the road and a journalist from the local Sunday newspaper who had heard about the bikes asked us for an interview. He told us it would be in the paper that Sunday and no, it wasn't the *News of the World*!

Bahia Blanca is a city located in the south-west of the province of Buenos Aires. The name literally means 'white bay' after the colour of the salt covering the soil surrounding the shores. It has a population of approximately a quarter of a million people and is a bustling hive of activity. The port has a depth of 40 feet, enabling the largest ships to navigate its waters and making it one of the most important sea ports in Argentina. It has one local and regional newspaper, *La Nueva Provincia*, and guess who would be in it that Sunday!

Che and Alberto stayed in Bahia Blanca with friends for a couple of days while they made repairs to their bike. But back then this estuary city was but a town and we wanted to stay in a town that hadn't changed since their visit. That town was Punta Alta, eight miles to the south-east.

We approached Punta Alta on the only road into the place, passing lots of naval personnel and soldiers. After riding around for a while looking for somewhere to stay we spotted the Hotel Valencia up a side street. It was the dodgiest looking place I had ever seen and I don't know how they got away with calling it a hotel. The proprietors were originally from Barcelona, an elderly couple who didn't have a full set of teeth between them. I expected *Duelling Banjos* to be playing in the background. It was a real family affair, run by three generations all mucking in. They were lovely people and allowed us to park our motorcycles on their interior courtyard. Unfortunately with the oil my bike was losing, the lovely terracotta tiles soon started to resemble black marble tiles.

The room they gave us was how I imagined a prison cell to be, except you would probably have been given cleaner sheets in prison. Compared to the field we had slept in the first night, the field won hands down for home comforts! As my head hit the stained pillow, the humidity, the exhaustion from the day's ride, and the couple of Stellas I had drunk that evening, sent me off into a deep sleep.

The next morning we decided to spend the day resting and doing a little bike maintenance. We started with a trip to a local bar for breakfast. *Lunas* (a half-moon shaped pastry) and coffee were the order of the day, served by a stunning looking girl who could have been Aphrodite, the goddess of love. Looking around we speculated that Zeus must own the bar, because the waitress serving the next table appeared to be Venus and behind her was the Egyptian goddess of beauty, Hathor. I don't know what was in the water in that place but it must have flowed direct from Mount Olympus. The DNA of those girls should be bottled and sold by Max Factor as a beauty treatment.

The girls on the streets were just as gorgeous as the ones working in the café and everyone was very friendly, as passers-by greeted us with polite *holas*. With its friendliness and its main street that resembled a Milan catwalk peopled with supermodels, we realised Punta Alta had to be Argentina's best kept secret.

We returned for both lunch and dinner at Zeus's place and yes, it was still full of Greek and Roman goddesses. The catwalk really came to life at night, as big American cars cruised the main street and jugglers performed at the only set of traffic lights whenever they turned red.

This was the land of the beautiful people and the only blots on the landscape were two motorcyclists from England and a hotel proprietor from Barcelona. We were just honoured to be allowed in the same town as these icons of beauty.

Walking round the streets of the small town of Punta Alta was like stepping back into the 1950s. Nothing could have changed since Che and Alberto had passed through. Punta Alta was also home to the Argentine Navy's largest base, Puerto Belgrano, and was where the cruiser *General Belgrano* had sailed from on that fateful day during the war for the Falkland Islands back in 1982. Testament to this was a white-walled graveyard containing row upon row of graves of navy personnel.

That evening when the heat had died down a little, we took the bikes down to the beach to say a final *adios* to the Atlantic Ocean. The next time we would see a coastline would be when, or if, we made it to the other side of this vast continent. And it would be a different ocean: it would be the Pacific.

We decided to heed previous advice and set off early the next day. After a short walk to the paper shop to buy a couple of copies of *La Nueva Provincia*, we discovered that we were now stars of stage, screen and the local Sunday paper, although the black and white photographs made us look like we were the original owners of the 1940s Nortons!

I gave *Kate* a tickle, a caress and she started on the third kick, which I was very pleased about in this heat. Pete looked at me and smiled, thankful he wouldn't have to tow me again. I was togged up, sunglasses in place watching Pete kicking, trying to start his bike. Then more kicking, followed by cursing and a little more kicking, before the heat took its toll and he could kick no more. Argentine hospitality stretched itself yet again, when two men who were passing started to push Pete and his fully laden Norton down the street. He swerved, narrowly missing the naval base bus and a host of cars before the Norton spluttered into life. We took the only road out of Punta Alta, the tree-lined road that had brought us into this Utopia. We noticed as we rode along that there wasn't an ugly tree in sight.

The next town on Che's route was the Patagonian town of Choele Choel, which sounded to me like some exotic Japanese sushi dish. It was a two inch distance on the map, so we reckoned a couple of hundred miles and doable in the day. Somehow, on the way past Bahia Blanca we got lost. We stopped to ask a local the way but he wasn't giving us any directions until he'd given our bikes the once over. He asked us the same questions we had answered a thousand times already, 'What year are they? How fast? Where are you going? Where are you from?' In our very limited Spanish and with a few hand movements we answered his questions, in exchange for some limited English replies and some hand movements, which I imagined had directions connected to them. A group hug, pats on the back and we were on our way.

My bright pink face baked in the sun once again; the open face helmet was very authentic but little help against the searing heat generated by the Argentinian summer days. I didn't know how many layers of skin I had shed since we had left the capital city, but it was of rattlesnake proportions and probably added to the dust clouds we endured, which were continually whipped up by the pampas crosswinds.

We endured our first drops of rain that day, all 12 of them, before somebody turned the temperature gauge up and the sun duly obliged, puffing up the clouds and giving them a designer cotton wool look. It was like riding into the opening credits of *The Simpsons*. We rode on and on, refreshed from the break we had taken. The Norton was running with a smooth velvety sound, a sort of chitty, chitty, without the bang, bang. I had grown accustomed to her and we were as one, man and machine together. She was a pleasure to ride and hadn't let me down once! Reliability was *Kate's* middle name. We rode towards Patagonia for what seemed like an eternity. We hadn't seen a soul or car for miles. The only evidence of humans was the roadside shrines and a lone truck passing. The highlight of the day was *Kate's* 40th birthday. Not 40 years but 40,000 miles on the clock, although I hadn't a clue how many times the odometer had read that figure over the last 59 years. What was true was that she had probably done more miles than the space shuttle.

We crossed the Río Colorado and were soon dropping into Patagonia. The brown open plain turned a little greener, with smatterings of broccoli-like bushes, dotted about the pampas, with no specific formation. We stopped to take a photograph of ourselves at the sign reading 'La Pampa Patagonia' and the driver of the only car we had seen in about two hours stopped to see if we were okay: such was the nature of Argentine friendliness. We were low on fuel and just as we were starting to run on vapour, a gas station came into sight; in fact there were two, right next to each other!

Choele Choel, was like a one-horse town that didn't have a horse. It has a population of less than 10,000 people and not a single one of them was on the streets. We looked for a hotel, but it was like a ghost town. We headed towards the Río Negro and passed row upon row of pretty pastel coloured wooden houses. There was a sign for a campsite, so we followed it, hoping to find civilisation. I envisaged Spanish guitars being played by Romany travellers in front of roaring log fires, straddled by suckling pigs spit roasting on locally grown pinewood skewers, while the women washed their men's clothes in the river on washboards under a starlit sky.

Pulling onto that campsite we could see the pecking order of the tents from the main house. The tents went down in size from the sprawling eight-mans with built-in Jacuzzis surrounded by potted sunflowers, down to four-man tents, which many a Bedouin tribesman would have been pleased to park his camel next to. I was the proud owner of a one-man tent still in the wrapper and hadn't camped out since I was a child.

I didn't even have time to turn off the engine before a litre bottle of beer was thrust into my hand. We were surrounded by families who were enjoying the delights of a family get together and an *asados*. An *asados* is the Argentine equivalent of the Aussie barbie, or the South African braai, except in most cases the animal is stretched out and cooked whole, for most of the day in front of a huge log fire, before being cut into smaller pieces and barbecued. It is deemed a real honour and privilege for an outsider to be invited to one of the family gatherings.

The two or three families surrounding us were all smiles, and questions about the bikes were coming from all directions. They invited us to join their *asado* and we were ushered over to the wooden tables and served with chicken, salad and bread.

The hospitality was overwhelming. We were given beer after beer, followed by as much meat as a carnivore could consume. Our lack of Spanish didn't seem to matter and we got by on smiles and the international language of Cerveza! We soon realised we were there for the duration and so I walked to the local shop to buy some beer. I was accompanied by a boy of about ten years old, who had taken a shine to me. His name was Marco (although everybody called him Marky). He had the dark skin of an indigenous South American Indian, a short shock of oil black hair and a wry, mischievous smile that had it not been on one so young would have given him the look of an assassin. Marky was very polite and reminded me of my sons when they were his age. We hit it off straight away, he helped me to carry copious amounts of Quilmes back to our new-found friends and he was my constant companion everywhere I went.

Mariana, the campsite owner, was a small, portly woman, with a thick head of long black curly hair, a smile that never left her face and a very persuasive attitude. She put our bikes into her garage next to hers and told us to pitch our tents near the *asados*. She introduced us to her friends Carlos and his wife Rosana, Pablo and another Mariana and Alejandro with his wife Celia. Between them they seemed to have a huge flock of children and they certainly knew how to enjoy themselves. I felt like we had been adopted and they certainly treated us like one of their own.

The first challenge of the evening came as I attempted to erect my tent. I use the term attempt, very loosely, because the tent hadn't been out of its protective sheath since it had left the factory. It was brand new, I had never put up a tent before and I didn't have my origami handbook with me. My whole newly adopted family was watching closely, as were my new neighbours in their huge tents as they peered through their plastic side windows and wondered how owners of one-man tents had managed to infiltrate the vast upmarket township of the eight-berthers. As I removed my tent and poles from their sheath I tried to look over at how Pete was doing, but his was nearly up and I had clearly missed steps one and two in erection technique for a one-man tent. Step forward my new best friend Marky, who hadn't left my side and was smiling at me. It was as if he was reading my mind. This young lad knew that I didn't have a clue how to put my tent up, my newly adopted family knew that I didn't have a clue and my new neighbours in their 'Super Bedouin eight personas' hoped I didn't have a clue, as they didn't want me bringing down the tone of the neighbourhood. Marky, with all the skills of a Tibetan Sherpa, laid the tent out on the ground. Within minutes he had stuck in the poles and the tent pegs were being hammered into the ground. The tent was up in minutes much to the amusement of our 'family' and the disappointment of the neighbours. I threw my bag in the tent, showered at the bath house and went back to the *asados* to carry on with the party.

That evening Rosana and her husband Carlos invited us to their house to eat. I had just eaten the equivalent of a full Aberdeen Angus and here we were being invited for supper. Of course we accepted, albeit reluctantly. The Argentinians seem to dine late into the night and we wanted to be away early in the morning, but hey, such was Rosana's smile we couldn't refuse.

Carlos picked us up just before midnight. We were quite tired but managed to exchange pleasantries as we drove the half mile or so to their house. Rosana greeted us at the door with a couple of beers and the huge smile she seemed to have patented. She was certainly my kind of woman and probably the most hospitable person I have ever met. 'Tonight,' she explained, 'my home is your home,' which was overwhelming considering we had only just met these people a few hours back. We sat round the huge dining table which took centre stage in their lovely home and were served different varieties of *empanadas* and beer. We were joined by Carlos's friend Sergio and his wife Christina and had a real, feel-good evening. Our common bond? Motorcycles! Sergio and Carlos rode bikes and were responsible for organising an annual mass motorcycle rally at the campsite in Choele Choel. Carlos and Sergio were enthused by our trip and had nothing but admiration for what we were attempting to do.

The drinks flowed and Rosana even showed me a new way to brew my mate (Yerba mate is a traditional Argentinian tea drink), adding a small amount of coffee and sugar. Then, Sergio brought up the subject of the Malvinas/Falkland Islands. You could have cut the atmosphere with an atmosphere cutter. I listened to what he had to say and obviously it was something that he felt very strongly about, as did I, but this was neither the time nor the place to have that debate, especially while under the influence of a dozen bottles of Quilmes apiece and numerous shots of whatever was in that purple bottle Rosana had been waving about! I soon twisted the *General Belgrano* to the Boca Juniors and we carried on until the early hours. It was about 3 a.m. when Carlos and Sergio dropped us back at the upmarket end of the beautiful campsite which nuzzled the Río Negro. Dogs barked and the glowing embers of a dozen dying *asados* fires lit up the site, as the nearly full moon skipped and reflected back off the flowing waters of the black river. To the Argentinians the night was still young – unfortunately we weren't.

I awoke to the sound of the flowing Río Negro and looked out of my tent but there wasn't a person in sight. The Patagonian winds had subsided and the sun illuminated the campsite on that beautiful summer morning. The cooking fires from the night before were still casting grey smoke skywards and birds sang their anthems to each other; it was a tranquil moment on which I paused for a time before shouting to wake Pete.

It was too early for most of the Argentinians, who had partied long into the night, to be awake so we paddled on our own in the river and admired the beauty of the place. We had our usual snack breakfast of cheese biscuits and water and then my friend Marky arrived. He helped me dismantle my tent and pack my things onto the bike. Marianna had also come to say goodbye. There were four of us stood around in awkward silence. Marianna tried to persuade us to stay one more night, but we had to move on. Then Marky did something that reduced me to tears. He gave me a small yellow T-shirt which he wanted me to sign with the felt tip pen he was holding in his hand. He had already signed it *para Steve del Marco*, I simply signed it 'Steve' and gave it to him. He handed it back to me. Marianna explained, 'The greatest thing an Argentinian man can give you is the shirt off his back.' Marky was giving me the shirt he had worn when we had first met. It was a very humbling experience for me. I gave him a hug, then dug into my saddlebags and pulled out one of my shirts, signed it and gave it to him. He gave me another hug, a knowing smile and then we left. I could compare it to the exchanging of football shirts at the end of a match, but this went much deeper than that. Marky had given me the shirt off his back and

I felt a real sense of honour. We headed down the track and onto the road to Neuquén. I wasn't leaving empty handed though, I was leaving with Choele Choel in my heart.

Chapter 6
La tierra de la leche y miel (y fruta)

Kate seemed to be humming a different tune that morning, something in the range of a Massey Ferguson tractor. It was a little cooler, which probably allowed her to breathe a bit more and she seemed a little more responsive.

As we rode alongside the Río Negro and deeper into the Patagonian valleys, the roads started to twist alongside the river. Taking sharp bends on the fully laden Norton was very difficult; it was like cornering a block of flats.

The climate changed as we got further into Patagonia and although the sun shone brightly there was a cold breeze that snapped at my face and neck. In no time at all we were both freezing. It was bizarre because when we stopped the bikes it was very warm. It was as if someone had opened the front door to a warm house on a cold winter's evening and let an icy draught in. The wind must have cut across from the Andes and over the Patagonian valley. It was almost sinister; it felt as if the Andes, even though they were hundreds of miles away, were calling us.

The desolate pampas we had left behind before Choele Choel had been replaced with lush green vegetation and as we passed through Darwin and then Chimpay we saw craggy hills in the background, jutting into the air like some old fortress protecting its domain. Once we had passed into the hills, they were replaced by trees in uniform formation, proudly wearing their medals of apples, pears and lemons. The fertile soil, along with the protective valley of the Río Negro, made it the perfect fruit growing environment. Even the roads became smoother so that the trucks carrying the produce to market would have an easier ride, causing less damage to their cargo.

On the ballroom-smooth tarmac surface we were soon chewing up the miles. Flanked by mile upon mile of orchards and vineyards, the town names changed to Indian names, Chelfore, Quequén and our destination, Neuquén. These names were evidence that until the mid-nineteenth century this area remained unmolested by the European invasion and, as Alberto Granado wrote in his diary, 'place names are all that are left of that indomitable race since armies of gauchos were sent out by Buenos Aires, Paris and London to "civilize the desert" and, while they were about it, kill the Indians and steal their land'.

Che and Alberto had spent the night in an empty police cell in a small town before Neuquén called Chichinales. We had arranged to stay with an Argentinian family via the couch-surfer's network, in the small town of Plottier just the other side of the largest city in the Patagonian district.

Entering Neuquén we crossed the river via a new iron bridge, which ran parallel to an old, unused wooden bridge. It struck me that Che and Alberto would have crossed the river via that wooden bridge and that it was probably the first time our paths had deviated a little since the start of our trip

Emi, the 19-year-old son of our host, Adriana, had driven down to the highway to meet us and show us the way to their house. He had smouldering Latin good-looks, with large liquid chocolate brown eyes and bronzed flawless skin, crowned by flowing soot-black locks of hair. A friendly smile greeted us when we met him with handshakes all round. He told us to follow him to Plottier which was only a mile or so away.

As we rode down the tree-lined roadway it suddenly opened up to reveal a huge Swiss chalet-style *estancia*, which had been extended and beautifully refurbished. It was a magnificent house with a real European feel about it; neatly cropped, sprawling lawns were surrounded by exotic trees and plants which seemed to go on for miles into the distance. The family's eight German shepherd dogs, including five small puppies patrolled and roamed the grounds in a playful but vigilant manner, setting off a chorus of barking as we dismounted our bikes.

Adriana welcomed us and showed us to a huge table under a massive walnut tree by the house. At the table were Adriana's husband Hugo, her sister Maria, who was visiting from Buenos Aires, a couple of family friends and the beautiful Elisa, Emi's sister, who greeted us with a smile that would have lit up a castle. Both children seemed to have inherited their mother's Latin beauty and their father's laid-back personality. High spirited and full of laughter Elisa had a rapport with her brother (whom she called Che) that would have put Laurel and Hardy to shame. This was the Partridge family and the Walton's all rolled into one.

The *asados* was roaring away at the edge of the garden and the wine was beginning to flow. The Catan family were captivated by our trip; El Che was a hero of theirs. They were enthralled, as we told them of our adventures over the last couple of weeks in their beloved Argentina. Adriana and Emi explained that they were off to Nepal on a two-month expedition later that year, so they could relate to our travel bug. Elisa was the unfortunate one, as she had to stay at home with her dad to finish her studies.

The huge goat's legs were taken off the embers of the barbecue, stacked on a large wooden plate and placed on the table. I was starving and reached over for the biggest leg on the pile and immediately bit into the inside of the leg … and into the goat's testicle which hadn't been removed before barbecuing. Not wanting to appear rude I tried to chew the offending offal, which was like mix of ear wax, phlegm and Evo-Stik adhesive with the flavour and smell of a dead skunk. I use the term 'chew' very loosely, as by now the roof of my mouth was riveted solidly to my tongue, which was in turn firmly glued to my teeth, by the offending piece of scrotum. The conversation taking place around me passed me by, not because I didn't want to join in, but with the testicle firmly jamming my mouth shut, I simply couldn't. No amount of wine was moving this reproductive organ from my mouth and it must have been a full eye-watering five minutes before I mustered up the courage to swallow and somehow hold it down. My appetite had dwindled and I nibbled at a celery stick to try to remove the pieces of tissue from between my teeth.

After the meal we were shown to our room, which was a beautiful open plan studio in the eaves of the house. It had a huge panoramic window from which you could see the orchards and vineyards for mile upon mile beyond the surrounding trees. It was stunning and, after the other places we had stayed since arriving in Argentina, pure luxury.

After a shower and a change of clothing, I had a kick about with a football on the vast lawn with Emi, Hugo and Elisa. It turned into an England versus Argentina game and with Elisa on my side against Emi and Hugo, normal service was resumed and England were solidly beaten by the Argentines. With a lot of taunts coming from the Argentines about Diego Maradona and the famous hand of God!

It was a relaxing evening; it was nice just to sit around the kitchen table and chill out with this lovely family.

Over the last couple of weeks I had come to realise that the Argentine people had a lot in common with ourselves and they loved to brag about that moment when Diego knocked us out of the world cup back in 1986. What did sadden them though was the war between Argentina and Britain over the Falklands/Malvinas and, as Adriana explained to us, 'There is still a lot of animosity in men of our age about the war for the Malvinas.' She told us that back then, when she was a schoolgirl, they had stopped teaching English in all the schools and people were told not to buy anything British. From an Argentine point of view they saw it as a one-sided war that they couldn't win and, as with Sergio that night before, I very subtly changed the conversation.

It was coming up to midnight and at one minute past the hour our Argentinian friends burst into song: it was Pete's birthday and the chorus of *Feliz Cumpleanos* (Happy Birthday) filled the air as I hummed along with them because I didn't know the words! We celebrated with pancakes, fresh cream and home-made pear jam, which had been made from fruit grown in their own garden.

We were woken by the dawn chorus of birds and yelps from the playful puppies at about 7 a.m. and our daily routine of bike maintenance and topping up of oil (which *Kate* was still haemorrhaging quite badly). Pete managed to repair his headlight, which had failed us the previous day so that at least we had one light between us. Our plan was that as we approached the police posts (that were at the entrance to every town) I would simply get up close behind Pete's bike and pass by on the blind side. We had a hearty breakfast of toast and coffee, and then it was time for us to be on our way. We were aiming to get to San Martin de los Andes, which was about 250 miles away, a big challenge for us as there would be a lot of hills, which would be a big test for us and the bikes.

It was a fresh but sunny morning and Pete's bike, which he had nicknamed *Cacafuego*, started on the first kick. *Kate* was having none of it and had to be pushed by Emi and Elisa before she burst into life. After lots of hugs and the customary two cheek 'mwahs' we set off, chased all the way up the track by the German shepherds snapping playfully at our heels.

After a few miles of riding, the roads soon returned to their bumpy best. It was like riding a horse in a steeplechase, the difference being that we didn't know when the jumps were coming up. It wasn't long before we started to climb the foothills of the Andes and once again the heat of the day was punctured by blasts of cold air. The landscape once again turned to rough pampas with craggy rocks everywhere, it was Marlboro country and the set of *Bonanza* rolled into one, all that was missing was Hoss Cartwright and Little Joe! The roads started to twist and turn, peppered with dead armadillos and lots of dead dogs. I very nearly added to the road kill when I narrowly missed a duck. It became great fun. The Nortons were responding to the challenge and any demands we were making of them. *Kate* was leaning round the bends like a thoroughbred greyhound on a dog track vying for first place. You could feel the pedigree, and for the first time my trusted steed and I were in complete unison.

We stopped for fuel and some lunch just after midday near a place called Bajada Colorada. The over-enthusiastic attendant filled the petrol tanks to the brim and as the fuel expanded, it crept out of the tank and on to the hot exhausts – our trip nearly went up in smoke. I treated Pete to a birthday lunch and then we were on our way again, pushing the bikes to their limit to make our destination.

Turquoise lakes brought the scenery to picture postcard life and, after hours of climbing, the mighty Andes appeared as a backdrop to the rolling foothills. Volcan Lanin towered over the others, its snow-capped peak looking over the rest of the range like some giant piece of Toblerone that had been topped off with toothpaste. We looked down on the beautiful lakes peppering the landscape. But the Andes majestically dominated the scene, proudly guarding the border between Argentina and Chile, a natural wall that separated these two nations.

We started to descend and weaved and twisted through this delightful scene, over rivers and past small lakes until we reached the Collon Cura River, which we crossed via a road bridge. Back on the 30th January, 1952, Che and Alberto had crossed this river by a ferry that ran along a thick steel cable which was the only thing that stopped the powerful currents from sweeping the ferry downstream.

After approximately 250 miles and eight solid hours riding, we finally descended into the alpine ski resort of San Martin de los Andes. Log cabins and alpine-style houses were dotted all over the coniferous hillsides. It could have been any ski resort in Europe; in fact the main avenue is called Ave. Koessler.

We soon found the campsite where Che and Alberto had shared a feast. It is run, as it was back then, by the Automóvil Club Argentino, Argentina's largest automobile association, which was founded in 1904. I pitched my tent in a time that would probably have amused my young friend back in Choele Choel and stood back in admiration. We were hungry and needed to eat, so we walked down into the affluent resort to find a supermarket, where we bought a couple of bottles of red Argentine wine, aptly named Norton, along with some beer, bread and olives.

We celebrated Pete's birthday on that fresh dusk evening, sitting on a log next to a stream that ran through the site. We ate and drank by torchlight until we'd had our fill, then climbed into our sleeping bags at about 12.30 a.m. As my head hit my inflatable pillow the hundreds of Argentine campers that shared this site, began to light their barbecues. Their evening was just beginning!

We woke very early the next morning. Pete was busy checking the bikes out and tightening things up and I was busy watching him! It was a cold morning, the sun was just rising and the warmth from my breath silhouetted against my expertly erected tent. We studied the map and our route to our final location in Argentina, San Carlos de Bariloche. This alpine city nicknamed, little Switzerland, made headlines when it became known as a haven for Nazi war criminals like the former official of the SS Hauptsturmführer, Erich Priebke. It was only about 120 miles away so we wouldn't have to push the bikes so hard, giving us time to ride the sinuous road of great beauty and take in the sights of La Ruta de los Siete Lagos (the Seven Lakes Road). At least that's what we planned.

We rode down through the centre of San Martin de los Andes to the shores of Lácar Lake. We were only about 30 miles from the Chilean border, but to stay true to Che and Alberto's route we had to journey south. We climbed the road out of town and took a final look back at that beautiful alpine village and the lake. It wasn't long before we were passing Lakes Hermoso and Villarino on that beautiful scenic highway. My chin was on my fuel tank, the scenery was so spectacular it simply stole my breath away! We stopped for a few photographs at vantage points along the way. The waterfalls, lakes and snow-capped mountains then became a blur, as we descended down the mountainside and the asphalt road ceased to exist. It was as if the local council had run out of money to complete the highway and suddenly we were travelling along something more like an old river bed. We only knew it was the road because we were passed by the odd 4x4 off-road pick-up, which was the only thing capable of handling roads like these. The Nortons weren't built for that type of surface, come to think of it not many bikes are. It seemed to go on forever and I nearly came off the bike several times, it was like trying to ride on marbles. I couldn't see for the dust clouds created by the passing jeeps and the bike was shaking so much it felt like I was re-entering the Earth's atmosphere.

As I dropped into a pothole the size and depth of a park bench, I thought my trip had come to an end. My headlight glass was in pieces beside me and my testicles were up somewhere near my belly button. I just hoped that this road didn't carry on to Bariloche, because we wouldn't make it. I managed to get the bike out of the hole and dust myself down. When Chris Rea wrote his song *The Road to Hell* he surely had this pebble road in the back of his mind somewhere! Pete waited for me a little further down the track and we had no choice but to carry on. After half an hour of trying to concentrate on missing potholes my mind began to play tricks on me and I began hallucinating, thinking I could see tarmac ahead. But there was no respite and the uneven surface carried on ahead of us. After another half an hour or so my speedo cable bounced up into the spokes of my front wheel and nearly threw me off the bike. By now we had missed three of the lakes as we were concentrating so hard on the road in front of us. After 38 miles of this, we hit asphalt once again. It was like rolling onto a gymnasium floor. I was shell shocked and thinking about suing the Argentine authorities for repetitive strain injury. It had taken us nearly three hours to ride 38 miles of terrain I can only describe as horrendous. We were absolutely shattered and still had about 65 miles to go. *Kate* looked like she'd been beaten. Her headlight glass was missing, the speedo cable was wrapped round the front of the girder forks and she was brown from all the dust. A mile or so down the road we stopped for fuel and were spotted by a coach party that had stopped for refreshments. The bikes took centre stage yet again and even though the supermodels didn't look their best, out came the cameras and guys who were normally at home doing jigsaws or Airfix models, queued next to the bikes to have their photograph taken.

As we rode past Lake Nahuel Huapi and into Bariloche, the beauty of the scenery didn't really sink in. The road we had endured from San Martin de los Andes had not only exhausted us, but taken its toll on our bodies and we were glad just to have made it to the lakeside city. We stopped at a petrol garage to call the couch-surfing host who had offered to put us up for the night but he was out of town and couldn't meet us until 9 p.m. which was a worry as I still had no working lights and darkness would soon be descending upon us. We headed for the city centre and parked up next to the main square with its beautiful lakeside clock tower. We then took it in turns to go find something to eat.

Pablo finally turned up at 9.25 p.m. He had come on the bus and lived a couple of miles out of town. We couldn't leave the bikes where they were and added to that Pablo didn't have anywhere safe to park the bikes at his place.

We decided instead to risk the 2 km to the nearest campsite in the dark. I rode so close to Pete it was like I was being towed by him. After pitching up on a hill, I climbed into the tent and immediately rolled to one side of it. The 45 degree angle of the hill was too much and I had a terrible night's sleep, trying to prevent myself rolling and taking the tent with me to the bottom of the slope.

On leaving Bariloche that morning of the 28th January, 2009, we felt a little sadness as we knew we were leaving Argentina, our adopted homeland for the past few weeks, and the hospitality of the Argentinian people. We had to follow the road we had used the previous day, as we couldn't cross the border where Che and Alberto had crossed. The pass through to Puella was closed, so we had to cross a little further north at Anticura. As we rounded Lake Nahuel Huapi and saw the ice blue lakes and snow-capped Andes in reverse it was just as jaw-dropping as when we had first ridden past them. The road bent and twisted round the lakes and would be able to host any road race in the world, especially with a backdrop of such beauty. *Kate* took the roads in her stride, handling beautifully as she munched up the miles to the Argentine/Chilean border. As we passed the sign for San Martin de los Andes, I looked to my right and gave an inner curse. That was the road that had tortured us the previous day and nearly broke our spirit and the bikes. But now it was onward and upward as the blasts of icy air let us know that on that sunny day, the Andes had us in their grasp.

The Argentine national flag was fluttering meekly in the windless heat, as we dismounted from our bikes and joined the endless queue to leave this beautiful country. The last time I had seen a queue like this was back in England during the bread strikes of the 1980s, but within two hours we had the necessary paperwork for the bikes, exit stamps in our passports and the Bariloche *aduana* (customs) had performed admirably, unlike their Buenos Aires counterparts when we had entered the country.

It felt a little strange when we left Argentina, like we were heading to a foreign country. As we wound up through the awe inspiring Andes the landscape was changing. The trees were a lush green and the piece of tarmac road in no-mans-land between the two nations was immaculately maintained. I wondered who looked after this stretch of road. Then up ahead we saw a huge sign which read, 'Chile 5 km'.

Chapter 7
Little England

'Bienvenido a Chile' read the huge green sign at the top of the hill we had been climbing. The Chilean national flag towered proudly above it, with the backdrop of the Andes reaching to the sky like a set of tramp's teeth topped off with Tippex. It was amazing – there we were in the middle of summer and those snow-capped giants still held many a winter past on their peaks. We stopped at the sign to join the queue of tourists who had just crossed the border and were having their photograph taken. Standing proudly with our bikes we painted on smiles while an unknown Japanese tourist pressed down on the shutter of Pete's camera and handed it back to him.

We rode down the fertile valley until we reached the checkpoint where we were told to dismount and pass through customs. We got the necessary immigration stamp and then had to have our bikes 'imported' into Chile. We had to wait a while until the paperwork was drawn up and once this was done it was time for the 'fruit and vegetable police'. There was a very thorough search of all our baggage for meat, cheese, flowers, fruit and veg, then a very helpful officer told us to pass through and into Chile. The only thing we were carrying that resembled fruit was some red grapes that had been crushed, fermented and bottled in Argentina under the name, Norton Red Wine!

The change in the landscape couldn't have been more dramatic. We had left the coniferous trees and alpine landscape behind us in Argentina and here we were, a few miles on the Chilean side of the Andes surrounded by lush green fields, deciduous trees, Friesian cattle and lots of foreigners! The fields were full of crops and it felt like we were back home. The tree-lined country roads could have been in the Lake District or the Ribble Valley back in England and all that was missing was William Blake's famous anthem, *Jerusalem*, as background music to this wonderful scene. The sign we had passed earlier should have read, 'Bienvenido a Chile (twinned with England)'.

Our initial destination after crossing the border was Valdivia, via the bustling city of Osorno. First though we had to exchange some money; we had entered Chile with only Argentinian pesos and good old British pounds. We left the beautiful scenic road to Osorno and headed into the border town of Anticura, a small town off the beaten track where time seemed to have stood still. Old, pastel painted wooden shacks lined the streets in this seemingly forgotten place, its beauty hidden from the many who never divert from the main road on their way to the bigger city of Osorno. The dominant feature on the landscape in this area is Puyehue Volcano, which can be seen for miles and boasts several hot springs and geysers and is one of the main sites of geothermal exploration in Chile.

We soon found a bank and changed a little money into Chilean pesos. The hardest thing was getting our heads around the exchange rate, as there were now 900 pesos to the pound while back in Argentina it was only 65 to the pound. A quick stop for food and drink and we were climbing the road back to our destination of Osorno. The sign at the side of the road read 'Luce 24/7', yet another country where you had to have your headlights on during the day!

Entering Osorno was absolute bedlam. The carriageway went from one lane to three, and cars seemed to come from all directions to fill up the lanes into this bustling city. Driving without due care and attention must be part of the Chilean driving test and it was every man for himself, with no shout of women and children first! We fuelled up and decided to head on to Valdivia to avoid being written off by the madness that surrounded us. After a couple of miles the road reverted to single track and the peace and quiet of the beautiful countryside was only broken by the beat of the Nortons' engines as we continued our journey north.

We were losing the sun as night started to fall and about ten miles before our destination we saw a sign for a campsite. Pete nodded at me and we turned off the road and headed up the dirt track. There were fields with three tents already erected. There were no facilities and we had to cross a rickety footbridge or ride through the small river beneath, to get to the tent area. The bridge didn't look very safe, so we had no choice but to cross the river. I steered the Norton through the flowing water and was grateful to stay on her, as she slipped from side to side on the shale riverbed and up the muddy bank on the other side. I was sodden, yet the bike had somehow remained dry. We rode up to the main house where we parted with handfuls of Chilean pesos (about £3) and in double quick time, pitched our tents as dusk became night. The heavens above looked as though they had been dusted with caster sugar as the stars sparkled against the pitch black sky. A chorus of crickets and owls serenaded us as we opened the bottle of red wine we had bought in Argentina. We made a toast and celebrated entering Chile. That night as I zipped my tent up for the first time on Chilean soil, I let my mind slip back to Argentina. I would miss the people, the *asados*, but definitely not the roads.

In the morning I awoke to find my tent wet with dew and the sun peeking over the horizon adding some heat to the crisp January morning. Steam rose from the pasture to form an early morning mist in the field we were camped in. It had been a while since I had taken a shower and as this place had no facilities I bathed in the icy cold flowing river. I then changed into clean clothes and washed my dirty, dusty clothes in the shallow flowing water. Job done, I felt brand new. After our usual breakfast of cheese biscuits and water we set off on our way. I left via our entrance route of the river but Pete decided to chance the old footbridge which straddled my morning bathing area. Revving his Norton he hit the bridge at about 20 mph. He managed to get to the other side of the river but the bridge, though remaining intact, seemed to follow his direction and was left leaning at an angle it certainly wasn't designed for.

We entered the city and commune of Valdivia which is located at the confluence of the Calle-Calle, Valdivia and Cau-Cau rivers and had been at the centre of the great Chilean earthquake of 1960 – the most powerful earthquake ever recorded. You can still find debris and destroyed buildings from the earthquake in the suburban areas but there were also row upon row of wooden houses lining the streets, exactly as Che and Alberto had described in their diaries. We rode through the centre of the city, the road edged with small lakes which had formed at the side of the flowing river. They were topped with an array of coloured water lilies which added a floral tribute and would have complemented any Victorian botanical garden. We had to push on though and headed out towards Temuco, the town where Che and Alberto had managed to get themselves featured in the daily newspaper, *El Diario Austral*.

We parked the bikes outside the offices of *El Diario Austral* at about 3 p.m. and asked to see the editor. We explained all about our trip and the fact that Che and Alberto had featured in the newspaper all those years ago. We were told that the editor didn't start work until 4 p.m. so we went to a café next door to wait.

The Café Austral was where the newspaper had been located when Che and Alberto had visited, but it was now a hive of activity of a different sort, selling coffee and pastries to the suited office workers of the surrounding financial district. We had almost finished our coffee, when the editor of *El Diario Austral* walked in and beckoned us over to the offices of his newspaper.

We got out of the lift on the third floor and entered the door marked 'Press Room'. The editor introduced us to an English-speaking female journalist and a photographer who, judging by the way his finger was caressing the shutter button, couldn't wait to get started on photographing the bikes. We were interviewed and between us, the journalist and the editor, managed to get an article together. Next it was the photographer's turn to hog the limelight. He led us down to the street, where a small crowd had gathered to admire the bikes. Grown men, again, waiting in turn to have their photograph taken with *Kate* and *Caca*. The photographer took charge and ushered the fans to one side as he took centre-stage and started to shoot pictures of us and the bikes from every imaginable angle. It was a scoop and he milked it for all it was worth. The following day our story and picture made the front page of the newspaper, just as Che and Alberto had done all those years ago!

Lautaro was the next place on our route, a small town which hadn't changed in decades. This is where Che and Alberto's Norton suffered gearbox problems and they had to have some repairs done. It was a chance for them to visit the local dancehall to let their hair down and in true Guevara and Granado fashion this entailed wine, women, song and fisticuffs! We managed to find the dance hall. It was located off Enrique McIver Avenue which was just past Bernardo O'Higgins Calle: evidence of the Irish influence in this great stretch of South America. It was boarded up and had iron bars on the windows. It felt eerie to be standing where those two young men had enjoyed a drink and a dance before being chased into the night by a jealous husband and his friends hell-bent on revenge for Che's advances towards his wife!

We had to be on our way as we still had quite a stretch to ride before we reached our planned destination of Los Angeles, the capital of the province of Biobío. This place held a major role on our journey as it was the final town Che and Alberto made it to on their motorcycle. If we could make it to this small town we would have made it as far has they had on their Norton!

On the long ride to Los Angeles I began to think about Che and Alberto's journey and wondered what had happened to their motorcycle that had made it irreparable. Ok, the roads were a little rougher when they had embarked on their journey and there were two of them on the Norton, but their motorcycle was comparatively new compared to the 60-year-old machines we were riding. Che and Alberto were both well-educated men and had planned their route carefully up to this stage. They both probably knew that in the next couple of days they would be reaching the mighty Atacama Desert, the driest place on Earth and a virtually sterile environment. It is blocked from moisture on either side by the Andes and the Chilean coastal range. The mountains, that reach as high as 6,885 metres are completely free of glaciers and some river beds have been dry for 120,000 years. To quote Alonsode Ercilla in his book *La Araunca*, 'Towards Atacama, you see a land without men, where there is not a bird, not a beast, nor a tree, nor any vegetation.'

This is a desert that is 50 times drier than California's Death Valley and occupies 40,600 square miles. Che and Alberto would have known that. What was in their thoughts? Did they have doubts about making it through that vast wasteland? Would they be able to carry the fuel and water they would need for this challenging part of their journey? Was their bike truly beyond repair, or had the journey through the hostile desert become far too daunting to these young travellers? Did Guevara or Granado nobble the Norton, realising it would be an easier journey hitching lifts by truck? In their respective books they mention that *La Poderosa* was making 'ever louder and stranger noises' perhaps this was the case, but we will never know what the real problem was.

My mind snapped away from these thoughts as a stinging sensation below my right ear went from DEFCON 5 to DEFCON 1. A wasp that had entered my open face helmet had begun to deliver its venom via the hypodermic syringe attached to its rear end. I cried out and stopped the Norton in a matter of milli-seconds. I removed the offending insect, made sure it suffered more than I did, and resumed the journey towards Los Angeles with the smile wiped off my face and my thoughts concentrating on the road ahead. We passed the stunning Malleco Viaduct, a bright yellow railway bridge which passes through the Malleco River valley and runs parallel with the twin lane carriageway we were riding on. To our right, the awesome stretch of the Andes watched over us. A great sense of achievement overcame me as we rode those last few scenic miles through Victoria, Collipulli and finally into Los Angeles, and I allowed myself another smile.

The first thing we did when we arrived in Los Angeles was book into a hotel. We had roughed it for the last fortnight or so and although it wasn't the best, it had a shower with hot water which was pure luxury to us! We had a celebratory meal and a couple of beers, which were far more expensive than we were used to back in Argentina. It made me realise why they call Chile the supermodel of South America! After dinner we set off to explore the town and to find Cuerpo de Bomberos, the fire station where Che and Alberto spent the night and the final resting place of their Norton.

It was about 11 p.m. when we found the fire station, a large royal blue building with big white doors. As we approached, a tall, smartly dressed gentleman, with a thick shock of slightly greying hair, was leaving the main door. We asked if this was the fire station where Che and Alberto had famously spent the night and with a warm smile, he introduced himself as Raul and invited us into the building. He was the commander of the station and showed us round. The guided tour started in the mess where we were introduced to Javier, the captain of Two Company and several other firemen who were all unpaid volunteers, as are all firemen in Chile! We were then led up a gold staircase and shown to the small room where Che and Alberto had spent the night. We were both moved by the sight of this room, it was so small and it was at this moment that it hit home – we were actually in the same place that one of the most influential people of the last century had slept. A red metal frame dominated the top of the stairs and held the large brass bell which had been rung by Alberto all those years ago and is still hand-rung to this day.

We had no cameras with us and asked if we could return in the morning, to take some photos and video footage. But there was a large convention at the fire station the following day and they would be very busy, so we nipped back to the hotel, picked up our cameras and returned to the historic building.

Carlo, one of the junior fire-fighters, gave us our second tour of the evening and showed us round the museum that dated back to 1888. It contains mementos of the volunteer firemen who had lost their lives; reminders of the dangerous job these volunteers undertake.

Once again Carlo showed us the small room where our pioneers had spent the night. It seemed almost biblical and then the daunting silence was broken as Javier shouted up to us that supper was ready. We sat round the table with the rest of the night watch and enjoyed a fried chicken dinner that Javier had prepared. It wasn't long before the banter started flying between our hosts, much of which we didn't understand, but we realised that the *gringos* were the subject of most of their jokes. These guys were certainly enjoying our visit; it broke up the monotony of their long shift and we were certainly enjoying being at this revered place. Then, the stuff every young boy's dreams are made of – two full fire-fighters' suits were brought out of the locker room. It wasn't long before we were kitted out in flame retardant hoods, trousers with boots attached at the bottom and braces over the shoulders, jackets, helmets and full Scott breathing apparatus. I was the stuff of every girl's dreams: a fully fledged fire-fighter. I even had a face to match, burnt bright pink, from the last couple of weeks in the South American sun!

We left Los Angeles fire station that night, to a chorus of sirens and a background of flashing blue lights. The volunteer fire-fighters gave us a rapturous send off. They were proud men, proud of their city, proud of their status as firemen and also very proud that a certain Che Guevara had spent a couple of nights at their station.

On leaving the municipality of Los Angeles early the next morning, we realised we were making a little bit of history. Che and Alberto's Norton had left this place on the back of a truck bound for the Chilean capital of Santiago. It was like we had been passed the baton and had taken over their journey. We were still under our own steam, although for the last couple of days, I had struggled to get *Kate* into gear. Her engine was also revving highly, but I just put this down to her age. Any mile past this place was a bonus. We had made very good time, and now our next destination was the city of Santiago.

We were determined to make the 310-mile trip to the capital in one day, which was a big ask both for us and the bikes. We had somewhere to stay in Santiago: some friends of Pete's wife, Michelle, lived there and had invited us to stay for a few days. This would give us the chance to take a well-earned rest, for Pete to do some vital bike maintenance, and for me to drink some beer.

Chapter 8
A new dawn fades

The Andes were vigilantly following us on our right as we started to put the miles under our belts. The sun was beating down as usual and vineyards stretched for miles and miles. We caught glimpses of grapes being crushed in the old fashioned way, by foot. What was rather off-putting though was that the majority of these old guys still had their socks on! My Norton had been vibrating for a couple of days now and was starting to worry me. After about 100 miles it suddenly shook violently and the vibration coming through the bike told me something was seriously wrong.

For some strange reason (apart from my very limited mechanical knowledge), I changed the spark plug. It didn't make the slightest difference. This was a problem with the gearbox or transmission and at the next fuel stop *Kate* was stuck in fourth gear. We hoped that if we put some oil in the gearbox it might just solve the problem. I bought some engine oil (they didn't have any gearbox oil) and put it in. The bike was still vibrating like hell and so, being the conscientious guy I am, I thought I would let it develop. Well develop it did. As we approached the next tollgate, my right trouser leg was full of petrol. I couldn't get the Norton into gear and the revs were stuck on full. I am a member of the AA, but this was definitely not in the home start package.

I pulled the bike to the side of the road and Pete took a look. The carburettor was hanging off and the fuel pipe was spewing petrol all over me. The throttle cable had also frayed and whatever the gearbox problem was could wait. Pete refitted the carburettor and undid the cable to sort out a direct feed: I had the cable attached to my hand and had to work it by pulling it manually. If we could just make it to Santiago…

We were 70 miles short of Santiago when *Kate* juddered to a halt, no drive whatsoever, she just stopped. We were now losing light and I knew we weren't going to make it. A passing motorcyclist stopped to help but this was a problem that was beyond him. Pete stripped the bike's primary case and pulled out a load of mangled metal which had taken the primary chain off its sprockets. Chain and case replaced we were on our way, but it was now getting very dark, the sun had set and we weren't going to make the last few miles into the capital. We pulled into a small service area, parked our bikes in a field, climbed into our sleeping bags next to the bikes and got our heads down for the night. I felt like I had slept in more fields than Red Rum, the Grand National winner.

Once again we were woken by the chattering of birds, but unlike the parrots of Argentina, these huge hawks were circling over us in a very unfriendly manner. We packed up our gear and after a quick coffee, set off on the final 45 miles of our journey. My Norton was clunking and vibrating really badly as we limped towards Santiago. A yellow mist that resembled mustard gas, hung over the mountain range near the city, which I guess was caused by pollution. A journey that should have taken us just over an hour took us over three hours as *Kate* got slower and slower. We climbed the hills towards our destination, and the Andes guided us into the city. We headed down Avenida Libertador General Bernardo O'Higgins but took a wrong turn onto Avenida Circunvalacion Norte when we should have headed for Avenida Americo Vespucio Norte. An easy mistake to make! Basically we had taken the outer ring road, when we should have taken the inner ring road. We were on the wrong side of the Chilean coastal mountain range and had bypassed the city. So we simply rode back over the Cordon de Chacabuco, a transverse mountain range of the Andes and dropped back into the city!

It was the last day of January and we had made really good time in getting from Buenos Aires to Santiago. The bikes had done amazingly well, but *Kate* was in a bad way. I wondered if this would be her final destination.

We eventually made it to the district of Viticura, an affluent modern area of the city and the place where our hosts Silvia and her son Ivan lived. We were afforded a very warm Chilean welcome with an accompanying ice cold beer. Following a shower and a hearty meal, we left the bikes for the first time since we had picked them up and spent the afternoon relaxing and gulping more iced beer on their patio. We were in a different world, a modern city like any other, which seemed out of place in what we had seen of the rest of this country.

Pete showed Ivan the map his sister, Tamara, had given us back in England to guide us to their home. It was no wonder we had got lost when entering the city, it was a tourist map from 1994!

Since entering Chile we had noticed that the people weren't as friendly as the Argentinians, they were stand-offish and perhaps a little suspicious of us. Ivan explained, 'The Chilean people feel like islanders, we have the Andes to the east, the Pacific Ocean to the west and the Atacama Desert to the north. We are a country that is cut off from the rest of South America by natural landforms. So unlike the rest of Latin America we haven't been affected by the European gene pool as much.' By this, I think he was trying to tell us that Chile was a little too far for the Vikings to rape and pillage! But there is a great Irish influence in the country. Bernardo O'Higgins, whose father came from county Sligo, was the leader of the Chilean Independence Army which fought and defeated the Spanish royalists in 1818.

Santiago is one of Latin America's most modern metropolitan areas; it has extensive suburban development, dozens of shopping malls and very impressive high-rise architecture as well as lots of bars! One of the things I liked about Ivan was that like me, he liked a beer or three. That evening he proceeded to introduce us to lots of bars. He took us from modern wine bars on to the bohemian student pubs in the older neoclassical parts of the city, which combined seventeenth-century palaces and art museums with modern skyscrapers and jazz music.

That night I climbed into the comfort of my bed a little the worse for wear from a mixture of Cristal Lager, Chica, which is beer fermented from yellow maize and a couple of pale ales. Ivan had certainly shown us that Chilean hospitality is as welcoming as any in the world!

We spent the next couple of days in this city of some five and a half million people, touring the attractions, drinking cold beer and eating copious amounts of bread, cheese, ham and avocados supplied by the very hospitable Silvia, who seemed hell-bent on feeding the two foreign visitors until they burst.

Pete then spent a whole day servicing the bikes and managed to sort out my gearbox problem. He gave both the bikes a tweak here and a tweak there, tightened up a few things that had vibrated loose and they were 'brand new' again. The only thing that was wrong now was the fact that my headlight didn't work. On a trip to the local hardware store I purchased a torch to tape onto the headstock of the bike. We also bought engine oil, which we were using in abundance, gearbox oil, duct-tape and bin-bags to keep us and our luggage dry when we eventually got to the rainforest. The only break of the day came when the local TV station, Emol TV, tracked us down for an interview, giving us 15 minutes of fame in Chile.

We left Santiago on Tuesday morning after saying goodbye to our wonderful hosts Silvia and Ivan. We rode from Viticura back towards the city and discovered an underground three lane highway, built parallel to the river, which avoided the rush-hour traffic of the city. The Costanera Norte is a toll-based highway system that passes below downtown Santiago and connects the eastern and western extremes of the city. It is pure genius: no traffic jams! In no time, we were back on the dusty road and heading away from the Andes for the first time since we had crossed them, towards Valparaiso, some 74 miles away. It was good to be back on the road. The warm summer air blew against my face and beneath me the Norton engine ticked away like a Swiss clock. I allowed myself a smile – the grin factor was back. This is what motorcycling is all about. Pete had worked wonders on *Kate* and she was performing just as she had when we set off from Buenos Aires a couple of weeks before. My thoughts ran wild again, we were going all the way to Caracas, we were going to complete this trip and nothing was going to stop us, nothing.

Unfortunately, something did stop us! Within a mile, Pete's Norton had come to a halt with a rear puncture. Repairing it involved removing most of the rear of the bike and cost us a couple of hours while he replaced the inner tube and blew it up with the hand pump we were carrying. It was our first puncture of the trip and a sharp reminder that things could, and inevitably would, go wrong.

We arrived at the seaport and resort of Valparaiso (which translates as paradise valley) just after lunch. It reminded me of a mix of Bridlington and Bournemouth, (with the smell of how you imagine Grimsby to be) which wasn't surprising as, during the late 1800s, the city had received large numbers of immigrants from Europe who had built their own churches and schools. It wasn't hard to see why it was nicknamed 'The Jewel of the Pacific'. With its labyrinth of streets and cobblestoned alleyways it embodied a rich architectural and cultural legacy. The funicular lifts, which are steeply inclined cable cars climbing the sides of the surrounding hills, are a sight to behold. Even the buses resembled the Victorian trams of old, running off the electrical cables above us. Valparaiso must be one of the prettiest places in Chile.

We headed to the port where Che and Alberto stowed away on a ship (the *San Antonio*) bound for Antofagasta in the north of Chile. Some would say that this is where they bottled travelling through the Atacama Desert, after realising it would be a lot easier to make this part of the journey by sea! This is the point where our paths would part, as we were heading towards the driest place on Earth on our Nortons!

Moored in the harbour was a superliner, the *Mariner of the Seas*. At 1,020 feet long and 142,000 gross tons, she was an awesome sight, a floating palace taking the rich and famous on the voyage of their dreams. She was a far cry from the ship our stowaways had boarded. Meanwhile I was taking my own journey of dreams on *Kate*.

We left Valparaiso and headed north on the coast road. The shining Pacific Ocean glistened to our left, as we climbed the hills back to the rigours of the semi dirt road. Trying to make up for lost time we were soon back in Marlboro country surrounded by huge cacti and drought-hit land. Above us, our first Andean condor momentarily blotted out the sunlight with its ten-foot wingspan. Its movements were remarkably graceful as it wheeled in majestic circles, not once flapping its wings. It just floated on the thermals to stay aloft and followed our path for a short while before disappearing beyond the vast, distant mountains.

Our guardians, the Andes, rejoined us and the harsh sandstone wilderness we were riding through was soon enveloped by a mist which seemed to be coming off the Pacific. It was a thick cold fog which penetrated my jacket and gloves. To our right, the world's longest continental mountain range bathed in the sunlight, unaware of the change in temperature and the fact that I was freezing. Then like someone had drawn back the net curtains, the sun reappeared, pushed the fog back and the temperature shot back up into the 30s.

Within a mile we were stopped by the Carabineros de Chile, the national police force. They checked our papers and were amazed that we were English. 'Why are you doing this? You must be mad,' was the comment from the senior officer. They were very friendly and after having a laugh at the age of our bikes we shook hands and we were on our way. Within a few miles we were stopped again by the men in green but this time it was two officers with a speed camera. It would have been something of a miracle if we had been speeding! Their colleagues had obviously radioed ahead and told them of two *loco* Englishmen on the Che trip. It was handshakes all round and we were soon back munching the miles. We had covered about 200 miles, which was brilliant considering the delay we'd had with Pete's puncture, but the day was closing in and we were in pretty bleak surroundings, passing only the odd, small village. We needed a place to stay. Then Lady Luck shone on us once more, 'Campsite' the sign stated. We turned off the road and headed into the wilderness down a dirt track flanked by ten foot cacti. After about a mile we came to a barrier and the entrance to the campsite.

Sherpa blood flowed through my veins as I expertly erected my tent in record time. Marky, my young Argentinian friend, would have been proud of me! We were pitched next to a tent which was the size of the Chrysler building. Parked next to it, was a BMW motorcycle and sidecar, with German registration plates. The portable stove behind the tent was the size of an AGA range cooker. These guys were certainly geared up for the great outdoors.

We were woken up early the next morning by our new neighbours, a German family from Dortmund. He was a tall portly man, in his fifties with straggly grey hair, wearing only a pair of oversized Y-front underpants which came up to his chest. A lit match burnt in his hand and he was about to power up the monster that was his camping stove.

'Guten Morgen.'

'Good morning.'

'Ah, you are English?'

The flame on the match in his hand was down to his fingers as he introduced it to the stove and it erupted into life. I was about to reply, but the ferocity with which the propane gas ignited must have snatched the oxygen from the air and I gasped for breath.

'Yes,' I finally managed to reply. 'From the north of England.'

'You would like coffee?'

'No thanks, I'm going to take a shower first.'

With that, he introduced what I could only imagine to be his burning fingers to the other rings on the stove and in no time had enough flames going to vaporise the Arctic! He then brought out a set of pans, as impressive as his tent, laid out like a socket set in a neat row descending in size, from a large cooking pot down to a saucepan. His set of frying pans was even more spectacular, laid out like a set of Jamaican steel drums. I hadn't realised they made them in that many different sizes!

Music started to come from his abode, along with the sound of children shouting and then a rather tall, elegant woman appeared from behind the tent door. It reminded me of the moment when Ursula Andress first walked out of the sea, at the start of the James Bond film *Dr. No*. My mouth went into 'goldfish' mode.

'Contzel, my wife,' the man said. 'I am Hans.'

I managed to introduce myself, but not to take my eyes off his wife: she was stunning! Probably in her mid-thirties, sun-kissed Mediterranean skin and long blonde hair. I made a mental note to purchase some XXXL underpants at our next stop.

After my shower, Pete and I boiled our kettle on Hans's stove and made coffee. It turned out that Hans, Contzel and their two young children, had started off touring South America with six other motorcyclists from Germany who had, one by one, gone back home.

'We want to see the south of Argentina,' Hans explained.

'San Carlos de Bariloche is beautiful, very German,' Pete commented.

'I have friends there,' replied Hans.

I quickly changed the subject to our trip. Hans sat there open mouthed as we told him about our journey. He was full of admiration both for us and the Nortons. His Praktica camera was soon at work, snapping away at the bikes. We departed the campsite after hugs and waves from our new European friends. As we left, Hans turned back to his cooker, with a lit match in his hand. He was about to put Calor Gas shares into the FTSE 100.

We were soon off the dusty track and riding onto the Chile Pan-American Highway, a heavenly piece of tarmac which would take us to La Serena, a town in the

Coquimbo district. The elements battled with each other as a freezing cold marine mist, known locally as *camanchaca*, came inland off the Pacific. But as the road went inland the temperature from the Andes seemed to push it back and the heat took over. It seemed like a crazy tug of war between the Pacific and the Andes, with no winner. The mountains were cloaked in a pure white cloud that looked like a white fingered glove stroking a black tuxedo. The Pacific was a beautiful azure blue on which sat a string of oil tankers waiting patiently offshore in the bay to unload their cargo. We had bought so much oil for the bikes that there must have been a shortage in Chile and they were surely here to replenish the diminishing stocks. There wasn't a part of the scenery on the trip so far that hadn't blown me away, it was all breathtaking.

As we approached La Serena we stopped for our usual lunch of chicken, bread and potatoes. Pete was having trouble getting second and third gears and his engine was misfiring badly. He added some more gearbox oil, changed the spark plug and that seemed to do the trick as the bike ran smoothly once more.

As usual, we hadn't made any plans about where we would be sleeping that night. It was just a case of watching our shadows getting longer until we knew we had about two hours before the sun went down. We always seemed to be riding on a wing and a prayer, but on these bikes we just couldn't look too far ahead. There were fewer and fewer cacti as we advanced. In fact, the surrounding vegetation was getting very sparse. We knew we weren't far from the Atacama Desert and as the road climbed steadily, the heat became unbearable. The dust from the arid land blew in small spurts across the road and I could feel the grit crunching between my teeth. The sun was shining brilliantly above us as we approached a sign which read 'Region De Atacama'.

Chapter 9
A big beach?

From that point onwards, we knew we had to get through a stretch of some 600 miles (1,000 km) of what climatologists call absolute desert. In the Atacama Desert there are sterile, intimidating stretches where rainfall has never been recorded. There are no blades of grass or cactus stumps, not even lizards or birds live in this remote place. The desert may be heartless, but it's a sympathetic conservator. Without moisture, nothing rots, so basically everything turns into artefacts. I didn't want to become an artefact and spend eternity in this timeless land – I just wanted to make it to Peru!

We were steadily climbing the slopes of the foothills of the Atacama. The roads were free of any type of vehicle. The only form of transport we saw was the occasional donkey. Pete's Norton had started to misfire and blow out thick, black plumes of smoke but we couldn't stop in the searing heat of the desert sun. Up ahead there was a building where an old truck had stopped to let its engine cool down. In the shade of that truck Pete got to work on his bike problem while I did the spanner passing (at which I had become something of an expert). We didn't know if it was a fuel problem or an electrical problem; Pete was struggling to find out what was wrong and it really looked like we weren't going any further that day. However, we had very little water left and we somehow had to make it out of the furnace-like heat. The driver of the truck and his mate came over to help but our limited Spanish made for a comical scene. There was an awful lot of finger pointing, shoulder shrugging, head shaking, smiling and finally stroking of chins when everybody had run out of ideas. Then finally, at about 7.30 p.m. we bade *adios* to the truckers. We were on our way. God knows what the problem was. I secretly believe Pete didn't know either, but somehow between him and the truckers they had fixed it.

Our next quandary was where we would spend the night. The towns were very few and far between and the blazing sun was beginning to disappear behind the hills. We just had to keep going in the hope of finding somewhere. We managed to reach a place called Vallenar, a sort of petrol oasis for trucks and coaches in the desert. It was already dark, I had no lights and we had nowhere to stay.

We had a black coffee and dry biscuits for supper at the fuel stop then parked the bikes on the concrete forecourt of the tyre bay next door. We took another look around us but this was it, our bed for the night. The rapidly plummeting temperatures made it very difficult to sleep and I shivered until the early hours.

I woke up freezing and in desperate need of a chiropractor. I managed to scrape myself off the concrete and had a bit of a wash in the sink of the gents. It was only about 5 a.m. and my bones were creaking. I didn't know whether to put my thermals on or leave them off, knowing that the sun would be beating down on me in an hour or so.

For breakfast we again had coffee and dry biscuits before we left the petrol oasis. A couple of overland, long-distance coaches passed us, splashing us with water which I hoped was from the air conditioning units and not the toilets those huge buses have on board. This was followed by the miniature sandstorm they whip up in their wake.

Ahead there was a mist. It looked like the clouds had fallen from the sky. We entered what I can only describe as freezing fog, visibility was nil and the cold bit deep into my bones. Never in any English winter had I ridden in cold like that and I tensed my body and gripped the handlebars tight. I immediately regretted my decision not to wear my thermals. It was a battle of mind, body and spirit as the ride became harder and harder. The sun had been snuffed out, it was as if someone had drawn the curtains on the day and I realised how powerful Mother Nature could be. I wanted to stop and give into her but carried on, battling against the elements. I was amazed at the number of roadside shrines we passed; surely all these people hadn't given up?

Two hours on and we were still riding blind, in the freezing fog. That bleak, unforgiving, bastard desert – how could the driest place on the planet be so cold? *Kate* started to miss the odd beat and all I could pray for was the sun. The next town was a place called Copiapo, but the mileage on the signs seemed to be going backwards. Then our prayers were answered. The sun woke up and dispersed the fog putting 'all three bars on the fire'. Ahead of us was a police checkpoint! I just couldn't believe it, there in the middle of nowhere two *Carabineros de Chile*, flagged us down to check our papers. With our limited, broken Spanish, smiles and their admiration of the Nortons we were soon on our way again without any problems.

After a few more miles the cold mist descended on us once again. It shut out the sun and the temperature dropped to polar levels. I just couldn't believe the adverse conditions of the Atacama. Then, as we neared Copiapa and descended towards the town, the sun came to us once more and stayed with us. The desert lit up in a scenic array of changing colours, from gold to brown, then to a beautiful emerald green, which sparkled in the bright sunlight (due to the copper ore content of the sand). The desert has very rich deposits of copper and other minerals, and the world's largest natural supply of sodium nitrate (Chile saltpeter) which was mined on a large scale until the German invention of synthetic nitrate in the early 1940s. The desert is now littered with over 170 abandoned nitrate mining towns.

By 7 p.m. we had made it to Agua Verde (green water) which consisted of a petrol station and a restaurant. I use the term restaurant very loosely as it was built from lots of pieces of plywood, cardboard and a door! If it had been on show in the Tate Gallery it would have been worth millions! We fuelled up and, as the petrol station closed at 8 p.m., the restaurant opened. On entering the cardboard café it became clear that we didn't need a reservation. There was me, Pete, a staff of two rather large Chilean women and a lone truck driver who had missed the opening hours of the filling station and so would have to spend the night in his cab before he could refuel in the morning.

We were given a menu but before we had finished reading it our food was served. Maybe it wasn't a menu. Perhaps it was a 'would you like to see what you could have eaten, if you weren't in the Atacama Desert' feature cut out of a long forgotten newspaper from one of the abandoned mining towns. What I did know was that the food on the plate in front of me resembled nothing in the pictures on the piece of paper which our waitress had rapidly removed from my hand. The trucker and the girls had the same: boiled rice and chicken must have been the 'dish of the day', or of any day that ends with a 'Y'. The meal was reasonable when washed down with a bottle of red wine (they didn't have any beer). My only bone of contention was that the 'chicken' had vertebrae and didn't resemble any chicken I had eaten before. It certainly couldn't have been road kill or a locally caught animal because nothing could survive here. Still it tasted better than goat testicle, and even that hadn't done me any lasting harm.

The two women came over to our table, interested and intrigued by the two *gringos*.

'More wine?' asked one of the waitresses.

'No thanks, but a coffee would be nice.'

We were brought a cup of coffee each, which looked like Marmite before you added the water. It turned out that the two things this café didn't have were beer and milk.

'You are going to Antofagasta tonight?'

'No, we are sleeping outside tonight, next to the bikes.'

'You will freeze to death in the Atacama,' they said in unison.

Leaving the coffee, which had probably set in the cup, we went outside and pushed the bikes around to the back of the restaurant, into the desert sand. This was a mix of nitrates and copper oxides, a very fine dust which seemed to get everywhere. With military precision, we unpacked our sleeping bags and climbed into them fully clothed. I stared at the night sky above. It was a clear night and a million stars lit up the desert; I had never seen stars so bright. Then the cold desert wind started to creep upon us, its icy fingers finding every small gap in my sleeping bag and wrapping themselves round my body. The waitress's words mulled round in my head, 'You will freeze to death in the Atacama.' The shockingly cold wind began to bite as the mix of the bright starlight and cold stopped me from sleeping. Daylight couldn't come soon enough on what was the longest, coldest night of my life.

I wasn't going to make the same mistake I had the day before, and with my whole body still shaking from the cold, I put on my thermal underwear before we set off on our journey to Antofagasta and then, hopefully, onto the copper mining town of Calama.

The desert looked stunning that morning. As the temperature rose I regretted wearing extra clothing and quickly discarded my thermals when we stopped for breakfast at a dodgy roadside café. Where those things came from baffled me. We could ride for miles and miles without seeing a soul then, out of the blue, we would come across a shanty building, with the word *Restaurante* hand painted in bright white emulsion on the side of a wall. They were basic, but a welcome sight on that long journey through the Atacama.

I found the whole experience of riding through that barren desert overwhelming. Looking out of the café door as the deep blue sky kissed the dusty sands I couldn't even begin to capture in words or pictures the imposing beauty of that landscape. It was how I imagined the planet Mars to be, desolate, yet surrounded by an aura, as the rolling red hills skipped away into the distance. I noted in my diary at the time, 'I have never known anywhere so remote, so bleak, so strange, or so cut off from the rest of the world. Its sheer beauty cannot help but capture your mind, your soul and your heart. It is a beautiful remote wilderness. This place will live with me for the rest of my life.'

It could also be a bloody cold wilderness, and as my hands and feet began to thaw, we set off towards Antofagasta. That was where our journey would once again follow in the path of our predecessors, who had disembarked from their ship at that very port. Che and Alberto didn't want to leave Chile without seeing the nitrate fields and copper mines. We skipped in and out of Antofagasta, and then rode right into the heart of Chile's copper mining industry, crossing the Tropic of Capricorn at exactly 2.15 p.m. local time.

Riding towards Baquedano, it was as if the desert had given up and died. Man had totally decimated the landscape and the scenic waves of the desert hills had been replaced by man-made mountains of tailings and waste from the surrounding mines. Industrial plant blotted the landscape, spewing out smoke and dust into the atmosphere. Sulphuric acid, used in copper processing, was being transported by road and rail; the stench of it hung in the air as it filled our lungs, making us fight for breath. We rode on and on, passing many abandoned nitrate towns where houses and buildings remained intact, like a land version of the Marie Celeste. Ghost towns, with brightly painted pastel coloured walls were well preserved in the driest place on the planet. We passed Chacabuco a town which became a concentration camp in 1973 during the Pinochet regime. It is still occupied by one man who lives there to honour the memory of the political prisoners who were imprisoned there. He considers himself a guardian, and guards the town to prevent vandalism and pillaging. To this day, Chacabuco remains surrounded by 98 lost landmines, left by the Chilean military.

We carried on along the mirrored road, the rising heat giving it a mystical quality. The scorching air stole my breath and burnt my nose. My gearbox was back to making clanking noises, but that was the least of our problems. As we neared Sierra Gorda, Pete was struggling to get his bike into gear and once again we had to stop. The gearbox was moving all over the place and it was impossible to make any roadside repairs so he simply jammed a chock of wood between the box and frame of his bike and we limped on to Calama.

Calama, whose motto is 'Land of sun and copper', is a town of some 150,000 people. It is a lively mining town, inundated by 4x4 vehicles (belonging to the mining contractors), with plenty of bars and restaurants. A hub of activity, the town is flanked by Chile's longest river, the Loa, creating a true oasis in the desert. We quickly found a hostel with safe parking and after being surgically removed from my pants we showered and headed into the centre of town. It had the feel of a Turkish bazaar as the streets were alive with street vendors trying to sell everything from fruit to mobile phones. We immediately found a bar and ordered two cold beers. I must have resembled Donald Trump with my wet hair swept back, because when I asked for the bill, the waitress had obviously mistaken me for the American billionaire and put the decimal point too far to the right. She was asking for the equivalent of Chile's gold reserves in payment for the beers. We had fallen victim to *gringo* rates.

I was awoken at about five in the morning by the horn of a train. Not the 'choo choo' you hear from Thomas the Tank Engine, but a ferocious claxon that nearly perforated my eardrums! The ground was shaking and I seriously thought the locomotive was going to come through the wall of our hostel room.

After a *café con leche* (they had milk in Calama!) a decision had to be made. Did we try to sort out the problems on our bikes here, or try to make it to Iquique, our next destination and the last major city before the border with Peru, and possibly our last hope for parts?

We made a decision and, with surgeon-like precision and me thinking that I suffered from obsessive compulsive disorder, I loaded my Norton in the same neat order I had for the last few weeks, bungee straps in uniform order and we were on our way. The bike maintenance would have to wait!

We headed for Chuquicamata, the largest production copper mine in the world and a major stop-off on the trail of Che and Alberto. This is the place they went out of their way to visit, to see how Chilean workers were being oppressed by the 'Yankee capitalists'.

Chuquicamata is, I believe, the place that had the greatest influence on Che Guevara becoming anti-American. Copper mining has long been the most consistent of Chilean exports, but mining the copper over the years came at a high price in human life. Testament to this is a huge cemetery near the mine. Steel crosses and iron wreaths cluster together, interrupting the vast landscape of dust. The rarely visited graveyard is immense and full of people devoured by cave-ins, silica and the dry desert. The desert offers them a certain immortality. Many graves have been looted, and the bodies blackened and shrivelled by the sun, lie uncovered and almost perfectly preserved a century after they were first buried. The still-laced boots looked quite usable and the desiccated remains of the miners will last for centuries, baking under the Atacama sun.

The mine itself is awesome. I can't begin to tell you how vast this place seems. The open-pit mine stretches three miles across and is half a mile deep. Fifty foot high dumper trucks, each carrying 360 tonnes of ore, look like ants on the giant man-made slag heaps as they climb up to tip their load. The town that was Chuquicamata is gone. A few buildings still remain intact but the whole town of some 16,000 people has been relocated to Calama so the land can accommodate this leviathan excavation. The one thing that does remain is the cemetery!

We headed up the one-way road towards the visitor centre, but it was closed. Perhaps visitor numbers had dwindled or nobody wanted to work weekend overtime so, unlike Che and Alberto, we didn't get to see inside the mine and left a little disappointed.

The sun was fierce as the intense heat once more began to bake the plateau below us. As we climbed the hills away from the mine I felt quite lonely and vulnerable, even though I was riding behind Pete. The remoteness of this land bewildered me and the oppressive temperature quickly sapped my strength. The only signs of civilisation were the telegraph poles supplying electricity to the mines. Even though it was a beautiful desolation, break down here and you would be 'goosed'! The road north was very quiet and it was rare to see a car or a truck passing. Further north, the roadside was once again lined with shrines. The last words of the majority of those to whom they were dedicated were probably, *Agua, agua*.

According to a sign we passed, we were 3 km from the next fuel station. After 15 km the mystery gas station appeared on the horizon, at a place called Victoria. It consisted of one fuel pump and a shack called 'El Oasis' (I called it 'Hell Oasis'). Again, I couldn't work out where the people who ran the place lived, as there was nothing else for miles. I had a cheese *bocadillos* and a beer to replenish myself, which also gave *Kate* time to cool down in the searing afternoon heat.

On we went, the Nortons munching the miles at the rate of about 35 every hour. Then we saw an optical phenomenon up ahead. Surely it was an illusion? But no, ahead of us was a true oasis in the desert. It was an amazing sight. There were hundreds of trees growing in a valley. The area is known as Pampa del Tamarugal and the trees are unique to this small area of Chile. The tamarugo tree is a flowering tree, which apparently grows without rainfall. It obtains its water from dew and only grows on saline soils. Within a few hundred yards we were back to arid desert and the road started to climb once more.

Before we knew it, we were looking down over the Pacific coastal city of Iquique about 2,000 feet below us. The spiralling road fell sharply down to the resort, like the road into Monte Carlo. Hundreds of cars seemed to appear from nowhere and the traffic was absolute mayhem. It was very difficult to keep the Nortons at a reasonable speed as we descended the snake-like road towards the city. I was stood up on the brake pedal just to stop *Kate* running away and the smell of the overheating brake shoes was overwhelming for the 30 minutes it took us to descend to Iquique.

My first impression of the city wasn't very favourable. The housing near the Cordillera was in disrepair and looked almost Soviet, but as we neared the centre of this seaside resort, the buildings took on a cultured colonial look. The two and three-storey buildings were built from fir wood imported from America and finished with balustrades, beautiful balconies and roof verandas to allow maximum light to the street below. The Georgian architecture was finished in an array of colours which would have brightened up any dark night. The harmony of sea greens flowed to peach then into mauve that reflected the sunlight onto the neat cobbled roads of this charming place, which takes you back in time.

By this time the bikes were getting very hot and we were getting desperate for a place to stay as we got knocked back from hostel after hostel. It was peak holiday season and it appeared the town was full! *Kate* was still making strange noises from the primary chain and Pete was struggling to get his Norton into gear as his gearbox was moving all over the place. Then we saw the words, 'Hostal La Casona 1920', and gave a reluctant knock on the door.

'Yes we have room for you,' was the reply to my question.

'You can park the bikes in the garage across the road, they will be very safe,' was the reply to my other question.

'Come in, I will show you around.'

Isabel Bussenius was probably in her mid-thirties. She had a baby face and her long dark locks were tied tightly above her head, giving her an added facelift. She had a smiling, fresh-looking complexion, with a scattering of freckles on her cute button nose and appeared far too young to be a hotelier. Her ten-month-old daughter was held tightly on her right hip. She showed us to our room which contained four bunk beds, a set of drawers and a bedside table. I chose a bottom bunk and threw my rucksack onto it to stake my claim.

Isabel showed us round the rest of the house and finally to the kitchen, where she poured us a beer. This part of the house resembled a Club 18–30 holiday. The kitchen stretched out into a huge covered yard where there were young couples of different nationalities, dancing and enjoying a drink before heading out for a night on the town. A smartly dressed duo from Colombia were swaying to the salsa music in perfect tandem. His high collared orange shirt and black stay-press trousers complemented his partner's flowing purple dress, which was hitched up somewhere round her waist as he sashayed his hips and bent her backwards. The music's crescendo made their dancing raunchier and it was as if they were playing Twister without the board. I didn't think it was possible for two people to be entwined together like that and I couldn't work out whose legs belonged to whom.

Isabel then poured us a welcome drink, a Chilean Pisco sour. This is a local cocktail made of Pisco, a local brandy, lime juice, egg whites, syrup, and local bitters topped off with ginger. It went down a treat and by the

time she was pouring us our third one, my head was
telling me it was time for my bed. The night was young
but unfortunately, I wasn't. As I climbed into the bottom
bunk my head hit the pillow and I drifted asleep to the
fading sounds of the cha-cha-cha and the mambo.

Chapter 10
The valley of death

Our body clocks woke us early, but it wasn't long before our dishevelled hostess, Isabel, along with her daughter, joined us for breakfast. I watched in amazement as she prepared coffee, bread, cheese, avocados and croissants, all with her right hand while carrying her young daughter on her hip with her left! She then proceeded to clean the kitchen, the yard and the rest of the house without once putting the child down. Perhaps they really were joined at the hip.

The rest of the people who were staying at the hostel filtered down through the morning, obviously the worse for wear after their night on the tiles. The Colombian dancer appeared, immaculate, with a high collared pink shirt and matching three quarter length linen trousers. He didn't need to give anybody the thumbs up, his peacock feathers were proudly stood up behind the perma-grin painted on his face. The synchronised dancing of the night before had been the ultimate foreplay and it was well after lunch before his worn out partner surfaced for breakfast with a huge smile on her face.

We took a walk to the shops and found the local ironmongers where we stocked up on engine oil, a couple of tools and other bits we thought we might need. Then it was time to do a bit of bike maintenance. Pete diagnosed the problem on *Kate* and told me I needed a new primary chain. The chain on the bike had become so stretched, it couldn't be adjusted anymore and was beginning to wear away the drive cog. So I left Pete to sort his own bike out and took a walk into Iquique, to find a motorcycle shop.

The city of Iquique is one of Chile's most visited cities and as I looked out at the warm waters of the Pacific lapping onto the sandy beach in front of me I could see why. The waterfront, where new hotels and restaurants stand proudly in front of the historic centre, was more than matched in stature and grace by the clock tower that has stood in the Plaza Arturo Prat since 1877. I had a paddle in the mirror blue Pacific and mingled with the tourists for a while in the 30 degree heat. The place is the perfect destination for a holiday as it hasn't rained there in over 17 years! I eventually ambled off the beach and found a bike shop; unfortunately it wasn't open on Sunday so I would have to wait until the morning.

Isabel had the night off and a young Chilean couple from Santiago, Ricardo and Paula, prepared us a typical Chilean dish called *porotos con rienda*. It was made from boiled beans and spaghetti and although it sounds basic, it was very nice. Then in true Chilean holiday mode, the Pisco sours were served up once again and, as the salsa music was cranked up, a certain immaculately dressed Colombian couple's feathers started to flutter at each other. The party had begun.

It was early morning and I was across the road from the bike shop staring out towards the Pacific at the surfers riding the waves, patiently waiting for the vendor to open up. We hoped to make it across the border and into Peru today and the only thing delaying us was the opening hours of the motorcycle dealership. 'Open Monday 9 a.m.' the sign read. It was now 9.30 and there was no sign of the massive iron gates to the entrance being unlocked. Perhaps the owner had been out partying with the Colombian couple the night before and hadn't managed to scrape himself off his bed. I was getting impatient but then, at 9.45, the rusty gates were swung open and I entered the garage and placed the chain off my Norton, onto the work bench.

'I need a chain, the same as this one.'

The mechanic looked at me, looked at the chain, then shook his head and gave me a bemused smile.

'I can order you one. It may take a couple of days.'

'I don't have a couple of days,' I said. 'I'm leaving for Peru today.'

'You will get shot in Peru,' the smile turned into a chuckle. 'The nearest place I can get a chain like that is Santiago, some 1,200 miles away. It will take a couple of days.'

The sun beat down on us as we climbed back up the snaking road out of Iquique. The sky looked like powdered sapphires, with the odd white, infertile cloud in the distance. I took one last look at the town below us as the Pacific reflected the sunbeams back at us like a giant strobe light. Then we were back into the desert. Pete had refitted the original chain back on my bike and the clanking noises that had been plaguing the Norton had resumed, giving me grave doubts that *Kate* would make it all the way to the Peruvian border.

To reach the Chilean/Peruvian border, we had to ride through the Seven Pampas. These are seven high desert plains separated by jagged sierras which form immense canyons, and the road through the sierras is very steep and narrow. There was also a fierce headwind to battle against and it whipped up mini twisters of sand at the side of the road as well as sandblasting my face. The sharp gusts of wind coming across the sierras, nearly blew me off the bike on a number of occasions and the heat was so intense, it stole the air from my lungs as I fought for breath. Even riding downhill, the wind was so strong I had to 'gas' the bike to keep it moving. We passed a sign for a town called Pisagua, which translates as 'piss water', which brought a smile to my face. The next town was called Pica, the name of the village back in Cumbria, England that I was raised in.

The sheer reddish-grey rock of the canyon walls formed a wind tunnel, as the mountains lifted high above us on both sides. The words of Psalm 23 jumped into my head for no apparent reason, 'Yea, though I walk through the valley of the shadow of death, I will fear no evil: For thou art with me; Thy rod and thy staff comfort me.'

This place was how I imagined 'the valley of death' to be. A lonely, hostile, and foreboding place. It was an immense wilderness that made me feel quite vulnerable. Then without warning, my Norton lost transmission and came to a halt as Pete disappeared into the distance. I knew what it was right away, the primary chain had finally given up and the split link had shattered into many pieces. This was the last place on earth we needed a breakdown and I thought my journey had come to an end. By the time Pete had realised I wasn't behind him and had circled back to me I had a spanner in my hand and had removed the chain case.

By divine intervention, the prayer that had entered my head moments before, or just sheer good luck (or all three), the chain had stretched so much, that without the missing link it fitted perfectly and once again, thanks to Pete's mechanical expertise, we were on our way to the last town in Chile, Arica.

With the late start to our day, the breakdown and the ride through the sierras, it was 6 p.m. before we entered Arica, some 11 miles from the Peruvian border. It was far too late to even attempt getting through the *aduana* (customs). The bikes were overheating and we needed to find somewhere to stay.

We passed the Morro de Arica, which is a steep hill and wound our way through the narrow streets to the centre of the town. The growl of the Nortons echoed off the dirty grey, rendered walls of the houses, turning heads and eliciting looks of admiration and envy as we passed.

Arica was like no other place we had passed through; it reminded me of the towns of northern England. The people seemed friendlier here and there were certainly plenty of bars. It was a rough looking town with lots of people milling around on the street corners and music seemed to blare out from everywhere. Once again our first task was to find somewhere to stay, with safe parking for the 'girls'. I left Pete with the bikes and went to look for a hostel. The first place I went to had rooms, but no garage. The second place was owned by a lovely elderly couple who told me we could leave the bikes in the reception area. They offered to clear the foyer, remove the glass table, the reception desk and the three-seater settee, which was occupied by two dogs! But I gratefully declined their offer, as the other guests would have had to climb over the bikes to get to their rooms.

As I walked up the street I could see Pete, surrounded by what looked like a gang of men. There were about ten of them, all in matching leather waistcoats, bearing the military lineage of their Hell's Angel rank. Underneath the winged skull emblem, were the embroidered words, 'Satan's Slaves'.

'We're gonna rip the town up man,' the first Hell's Angel roared as we exchanged a ghetto handshake and high fives. 'Yeah, Armageddon tonight,' said a second, in a slightly camp tone, giving me a limp handshake. He was wearing a red bandana that only just hid his 'comb over' hairstyle. 'We'll drink the town dry,' a third added giving me a bear hug while still wearing his German helmet fastened tightly under his chin, as the handshakes continued round the group.

On closer inspection, with their neatly trimmed beards, matching cowboy boots and shiny leathers, they weren't the rock hard lads they had first appeared. I couldn't imagine they had even heard of The Grateful Dead, let alone bitten a chicken's head off. In fact, they wouldn't have looked out of place at a Barry Manilow appreciation society meeting. Perhaps the Spanish writing, embroidered on their backs had been mistranslated in my mind and what I had at first read as 'Satan's Slaves', was in fact 'Santa's Elves'? Nonetheless, we were fellow motorcyclists and with the British bikes and mix of oil and sand on our clothing, we were a match for any of these 'greasers'.

They told us they were from Santiago and were camping out on the beach. I automatically assumed from their attire that they had bikes and hadn't come here on the bus, and we arranged to meet them at about 10 p.m. to 'drink the place dry'! We then left them outside the bar in which we were to meet and went to look for a place to stay.

As we rode towards the neon sign reading 'Hostal Francais', Pete's clutch cable snapped and he had to push *Caca* the final ten yards or so to the hostel. It had been a long, hard day's ride and the snapped cable repair was a job that would have to wait until the morning. The French expatriate proprietor of the hostel showed us to our room as it was away from the main house with a secure parking area for the bikes. We quickly showered, found a nearby café for our usual fix of chicken and chips and then went to the bar where we had arranged to meet our brothers of the road.

After an hour and a couple of beers they hadn't arrived. We decided to walk up the beach road to see if we could find where they were camping, but with more than 20 km of beaches, we didn't have a chance. We went back to the bar for a couple more beers and at around midnight, unlike the rest of Chile the place started to close down. There would be no Armageddon tonight. 'Santa's little helpers' were probably tucked up in their tents wearing matching leather pyjamas, drinking hot cocoa and listening to Barry Manilow's greatest hits. We made our way back to the hostel and I climbed wearily into my bed. I was a little apprehensive, as we would be crossing into Peru the following day. 'You will get shot in Peru,' I had been told.

The following day we walked into town to buy a soldering iron to repair Pete's clutch cable. It was Tuesday 10th February and we had been on Chilean soil for 13 days. It had taken Che and Alberto 38 days to pass through Chile. They had stopped over at the same towns, but had been reliant on trucks and cars to get them to their destination, having left their Norton in Santiago. Our Nortons seemed to be holding up pretty well and we had a renewed optimism that we could go all the way on the bikes.

Unable to purchase a soldering iron Pete once again worked his magic, using the camping stove, a pair of pliers and some solder to repair his clutch cable. We did about an hour of maintenance on the bikes, including the daily topping up of the oil reservoir. The bikes were loaded up and we were ready to go.

We headed out of Arica towards the border with Peru and were immediately thrust back into a desert landscape and the horrendous crosswinds we had endured for the last couple of days. After about a mile, *Kate* suddenly sounded like a Lancaster bomber. I immediately pulled her over to the side of the road to discover my exhaust had parted company with the cylinder head. Wearing my thick leather gloves I managed to screw the exhaust outlet pipe back onto the thread on the cylinder head and I was back up and running. I learned a valuable lesson from this episode: looking down at the singed holes in the palms of my gloves I discovered that leather does burn!

When we arrived at the Chilean border post we joined the customary queue. When we eventually reached the window, we were told that we hadn't filled in the correct form. After filling in the correct form we approached the sign thanking us for visiting Chile, only to be told we needed more stamps on it. It had taken us about an hour and a half to get all the right paperwork together and with one more stamp we could leave Chile.

We handed the completed documentation to the final checkout post and as we passed the 'Bienvenidos' sign we entered the no-man's-land between the two countries which was littered with signs reading, 'Minas' to warn us of the landmines that were laid in the fields between the two countries.

Chapter II
The land of the Incas

We were welcomed to Peru by a very friendly border guard who pointed us in the direction of the customs building. The Customs and Immigration officers were very professional and within an hour they had broken all South American import records and we were on Peruvian soil.

The huge red and white Peruvian flag flapped wildly in the wind as we walked towards our bikes and mounted them. At the moment we were due to leave, a cortege of gleaming Chinese-built motorcycles arrived at the customs building. It was the Armageddon boys from Arica. We gave them a polite wave as we set off. Peru was two hours behind Chilean time and with no lights on my bike we had to get on. It would be dark by 6 p.m.

The first place we reached was the city of San Pedro de Tacna, or simply Tacna. It's about 22 miles north of the border with Chile and was a madhouse, where it seemed compulsory to have your hand slammed down hard on the horn of your vehicle at all times. Mixed with the loud shrill of whistles blown by policemen stopping traffic at every crossing, the noise was deafening. Pedestrians seemed to leap in front of me like suicidal lemmings at every opportunity and after the tranquillity of riding through the desert, this place was absolute mayhem.

The Peruvians' skin colour was noticeably darker than the Chileans, which stemmed from the Ayamara and Quechua influence of the region. These tribes were the original inhabitants of Peru some 2,000 years ago, before being conquered by the Incas. The women we saw were all dressed in brightly coloured national dress, wide layered petticoats with ponchos and traditional bowler hats. It was as if we had entered a different world.

Tacna was a mix of old and new buildings, which all seemed to be painted white. We passed the beautiful neo-Renaissance cathedral, with its huge dome, flanked proudly by twin bell towers. In front of it was the arch of the Alto de la Alianza, which commemorates a crucial battle which took place between an alliance of Bolivian and Peruvian forces against the Chileans on 26th May, 1880, resulting in the city being Peruvian!

After changing what little Chilean pesos we had left into Peruvian sols, we refuelled, tried unsuccessfully to buy a road map of Peru and somehow navigated our way out of the city. Our intention was to get as far into Peru as possible with what little daylight hours were left. We passed another beautiful white building topped by a large dome and high towering minaret which was the Mosque of Bab ul Islam. It is the only Islamic structure in the whole of Peru and you can imagine why: there is no way the muezzin's call to prayer could be heard above the din of the traffic and the whistling police! The cathedral, with its huge bell towers, had the right idea.

There were no road signs so we got lost up a dirt track and had to ride back through the noisy city and ask for directions. We eventually picked up the road to Moquegua which helter-skeltered up the hills out of Tacna. The ride was great except for the strong winds, which slowed us down and did their utmost to blow us off the bikes. After a couple of hours we dropped into lush green valleys, with vines, olives and beautiful coloured flowers. There were lemons, limes and apricots filling the fields adjacent to the road, herds of cows and goats grazed and for the first time in a few days I was hit in the face by flies, a sure sign we were out of the desert! The ride became pleasurable once more. The smell of the land and the greenery entered my nostrils and there was now something to gaze at apart from miles and miles of barren wilderness. The next thing was to find somewhere to stay as the sun was starting to drop below the distant mountains, and the shadows of the bikes stretched further away from us.

Then out of nowhere a wooden shack at the side of the road appeared, with the hand painted word *Hostal* scrawled on the walls. I nodded at Pete; this would be our bed for the night. I imagine we caught them 'out of season' as we were the only guests, but after a chicken and chip supper and a very sweet bottle of Peruvian wine we were tucked up in our beds and asleep by 8.30 p.m. Our body clocks were still on Chilean time.

We were up exceptionally early on the morning of the 11th February. We left the hostel at about 6.15 a.m. and set off on our way to Puno. The full moon still dominated the vast pale blue sky and as the sun ascended from behind the remote black mountains it gave the fertile land a rusty red look. Individual cattle on their way to be milked at a small roadside shed were being walked along the side of the road by small boys and traditionally dressed women. This place was idyllic.

We refuelled on the outskirts of Moquegua on the usual low grade *sin plomb* and the pump attendant reassured us that the road that led to Puno was accessible on the bikes. With rimmed tanks, we were on our way, chased out of town by a couple of dogs and guided by Pete's 1950s Esso map!

The road out of Moquegua climbed upwards at an alarming rate and the countryside started to become desolate. We were waved through the small villages of Samegua, Torata and Chillihua by smiling Peruvian children who seemed bewildered by the bikes, before being chased out of the villages by packs of pursuing dogs.

The road snaked upwards round the mountains and the higher we climbed the lower the temperatures dropped. The little asphalt that had been on the roads earlier disappeared, having been washed away by the rain that cascades down the mountains, and all that remained could be described as a farm track or dirt road.

We had set off in relatively warm sunshine and now the cold began to bite at my face and leather-gloved hands. My bike had started to miss the odd beat and I was going through the gears to keep her going as the cold air became thinner and thinner, affecting her performance. I wondered if *Kate* was going to make it. The road continued to climb and climb until we reached a sign telling us we were 12,500 feet above sea level. At this point my whole body stiffened up with the cold. The scenery was stunning, there were snow-capped mountains in the distance and grazing llamas and donkeys peppering the sparse fields, but the cloud above us thickened and turned black and the freezing temperatures gripped me like a vice. We reached about 15,500 feet and it became unbearable. My teeth chattered and my whole body ached with the rigidity it had endured for the last couple of hours climbing that mountain, I even tried riding along alternating my hands against the cylinder head, just to get some warmth into them, but the cold air was the only winner at that altitude.

In Chile the Andes had been a constant riding companion, guiding us through the country, but in Peru they enveloped us. The Andes were about to become a big challenge for us and the bikes. We had been riding for two and a half hours and only managed to cover 38 miles!

High up on the pass we came across two traditionally dressed Peruvian women outside two small wooden shacks selling fruit and popcorn. We stopped and I asked if they sold coffee and the answer, thankfully, was *si*.

We entered one of the sheds and sat down on a wooden bench which was covered with a moth-eaten llama skin rug. The loose dirt floor was uneven and the table we sat at wobbled from side to side at the slightest touch. We were surrounded by locals eating from big bowls of what I can only describe as pea and ham soup without the pea and ham! The green water steamed in the cold air and didn't look at all appetising. But we ordered two bowls of it anyway, not through hunger but because it seemed that was the only thing that they served and we hoped it would thaw us out. The soup arrived along with cups of the black asphalt they tried to pass off as coffee and we gratefully demolished the lot.

Pete gasped for breath and complained of feeling nauseous and light headed and I realised that the altitude was starting to affect him. We set off once again on the winding mountain pass, shivering round the hairpin bends which were signed 'Curva Peligrosa' (dangerous bend). The only traffic we saw was the odd fuel tanker coming the other way, usually on our side of the road so we just hugged the outside of the mountain road to avoid being wiped out. There were no crash barriers here, just sheer drops into the ravines below that would mean certain death if you left the road.

The black clouds ahead seemed to be coming towards us, making a stunning backdrop to the huge snow-capped volcano (Tutpaca) which reached 18,963 feet. Then a hailstorm hit us. The black clouds had arrived and dispersed their icy pellets over the mountain. My wind-chafed face was now stinging as the hailstones rattled into me and my only defence was to put my goggles down, scream out loud with numerous swear words and keep going. The storm subsided for a while as we passed through the village of Humajalso and on towards our destination, Puno. The hours were passing quickly as the Nortons struggled with the thin air and we covered far fewer miles than we had anticipated.

We soon discovered that in Peru fuel stations are restricted to the bigger towns and cities. In the smaller villages, local people sold it from their houses to make some money; we just had to look out for the word *gasolina* painted on signs at the roadside. We refuelled at a house in Santa Rosa and also had a coffee in the owner's living room, where we managed to thaw out a little. We were given a send-off like we were long-lost friends. Later, when we were stopped for the first time by a policeman at a toll-gate he simply shook our hands and smilingly waved us on our way.

As the landscape flattened out a little, the asphalt returned and we started to pick up the pace again. The only thing that slowed us was the return of the hailstorm as we passed through Mazo Cruz, a small town which seemed to be the biggest truck stop in the world, with dozens of trucks lined three abreast along the side of the road. We were cold and soaked to the skin but carried on, as the road descended once more and the pastures came back. Sheep and llamas were being tended in the fields by women and children and a snake slithered across the road in front of me, which shocked me. Further on I was nearly knocked off the bike by a few sheep, which decided to cross the road as I was passing. It was very hazardous riding, but also fun and took my mind off my freezing state.

As we went further dry stone walls and fields full of crops appeared. Oxen pulled wooden ploughs through the muddy fields and I realised that this place hadn't changed in hundreds of years.

We rode alongside Laguna Winaymarca (which forms a border with Bolivia) towards Zepita. Then before we knew it, we were riding next to Lake Titicaca, which at 12,500 feet above sea level is the highest navigable lake in the world and by water volume, the largest lake in South America. The Bolivian Navy actually use the lake to carry out naval exercises, maintaining an active navy despite being landlocked! Fishermen had their nets stretched out along the shores and many women worked the land next to the lake, farming potatoes and beans in the sodden fields. That area was a male chauvinist's paradise and I'm sure many of the women working that land must have been given a wheelbarrow as a birthday gift!

When we entered Puno I smiled, half expecting to be wiped out by the traffic of taxis, rickshaws and tuk-tuks that were all fighting for the same road space as us. With their hands on their horns and claxons they gave us what seemed like a fanfare entrance to the city, as we weaved in and out of the pandemonium. We parked the bikes as near as we could to the centre of town and as Pete was still feeling a little under the weather I set off on foot to try to find somewhere to stay while he looked after the bikes.

If the Ayamara tribe still exists anywhere, then it is in Puno. The dark skin of the Andean Indians made me stand out like Martin Luther King at a Klu Klux Klan meeting and I turned heads wherever I walked as I looked for a place to stay.

It took me over an hour to find a hostel as there was some kind of festival going on in the town, but after being assured that the room had hot water (a luxury on this trip) I handed over the 30 sol (about £7) for the room and went to get Pete and the bikes. The altitude was still affecting Pete, but we were hungry and in desperate need of food, so after parking the bikes in the hostel's garage, we headed straight into the cauldron of noise and car horns that is Puno.

I was sick of eating chicken and chips, it was all I had eaten for the last couple of weeks, so we decided to break with tradition and get a pizza (although guinea pig was on the menu!). The Machu Pizza Restaurante was where we sampled the thin crusted culinary delight that originated in Italy, and we weren't disappointed as the Trujillo beer flowed and the hot vegetable pizza was served.

We had arrived in Puno during the festival of the Virgen de la Candelaria which more than 200 groups of musicians and dancers had gathered to celebrate. The streets were heaving with brass bands, pan pipes and dancers clad in spectacular costumes and outlandish masks to celebrate their offerings to the Incan earth goddess Pachamama. The festival is a Christian one but linked to pre-Hispanic times and the agricultural cycles of sowing and harvesting as well as mining activities and is a mix of respectful Ayamara gaiety and ancestral Qeuchua seriousness. Believe it or not, the dancers and bands who fill the streets finally head to the cemetery to pay homage to the dead!

We watched as the bands and dancers filed past us and realised that it was going to go on well into the night. It had been a very long day and the ride had taken its toll on us so we decided to head back to the hostel. The altitude had taken hold of Pete and he was struggling for breath as we got back to our room. A hot shower was out of the question as, surprise, surprise, there was no hot water in the room, and a good night's sleep was a definite no as the festival raged on in the streets outside!

The all night disco that had started up in the bar next to our hostel to mark the festival woke me at about 5.30 a.m. Queen's *Radio Ga Ga* blared from a tinny amplifier and the words were drowned out as the revellers clapped in unison to, 'All we can hear is Radio ga ga.' Clap, clap! 'Radio goo goo,' followed by louder clapping. I was in desperate need of a shower and escape from the mind numbing anthem going on below. I turned on both taps in the shower, only to be served with freezing cold water from both. I went down to reception wrapped in my small travel towel, to complain that there was no *agua caliente* (hot water). The guy in reception just smiled at me and nodded, 'caliente, caliente,' he repeated. I couldn't be bothered to argue with him so early in the day, so I went back up to the room, got dressed and went for a walk round the town.

I walked to the Plaza de Armas, dominated by the magnificent Cathedral of Puno, passing several Spanish colonial churches on my way. Bands were still playing in the square outside the cathedral. I was absolutely knackered with both lack of sleep and the arduous journey of the day before and I walked in a daze as if I was on auto-pilot.

Back at the hostel, Pete was still in bed and feeling ill. He hadn't slept very well and was complaining of light-headedness and disorientation. There was no way we could travel on the bikes that day; he was fatigued and any physical exertion was out of the question. Besides we hadn't been to see Lake Titicaca, a place Che and Alberto described as a 'milestone' on their journey and, according to Incan mythology, the place the world was created from when the god Viracocha came out of the lake.

'Diamox,' was the answer Pete got when he asked the lady serving in the pharmacy about his altitude sickness and after parting with a few sols he had the answer to his prayers. By mid-afternoon Pete was feeling a little better. The brass bands and dancers were parading the packed streets once more, so we decided to walk down to the shores of Lake Titicaca.

We headed towards the lake, passing through wet, muddy streets where poverty was rife. Many of the people wore no shoes and the shoddy housing was in a state of disrepair. The one thing that these people did wear with pride though was a huge smile. Walking towards the lake at first felt a little intimidating, but the warm smiles that were directed our way put me at ease. When we reached the lake we were approached by a man with owl-like eyes the colour of burnt toast. He sported a thick, soot-black handlebar moustache which almost touched the epaulettes of his navy wool jacket, which was complemented by a pair of white boating plimsolls.

'You want a boat to the Uros?' the man asked as his eyes rolled towards the moored boats behind him.

'How much?' I replied.

'Eighty sols,' (about £18) he smiled a little, but the huge moustache never moved.

'Forty sols,' Pete interrupted, and before another word could be said, our captain had ushered us towards a small motor launch, happy with the deal.

There are contrasting reports in Che Guevara and Alberto Granado's diaries as to whether they got out onto the lake. Alberto explained that it was impossible to get out on the water as they couldn't make themselves understood to the local fishermen. Che mentions using an interpreter to speak to the Ayamara fishermen who, he says, took them out onto the lake for the modest sum of five sols. Conflicting entries, yet neither of them mention the Uros, a group of 42 or so floating islands that are made of totora reeds which grow in the shallows of the lake.

There was only me and Pete on the boat and I asked the captain if I could take over the wheel. With nothing else on the lake at that point I took over the helm and made a course for the Uros Islands. In the distance to our left was the rusting hulk of a lavish steam cruiser of yesteryear, which had been built in England and was once used for luxury cruises round this vast lake.

Stepping onto the man-made reed islands of the Uros was like treading onto a giant mattress as the islands move underfoot. The original purpose of the island settlements was defensive: if a threat arose they could be moved round the huge lake. Some of the larger islands house up to ten families in dwellings made of the same reeds as the islands; their boats are made from reeds as well. The local people were selling their wares of handmade jewellery, clothing and refreshments and it felt truly authentic, like we had stepped back into a bygone age. That was until I heard the famous Nokia ring-tone and one of the traditionally dressed Uros women answered the mobile phone she had in her petticoat. It was probably a call from her stockbroker!

The following morning we were up early and after a cold shower, we decided to go and visit the British-built steamships we had seen and that Che had mentioned in his journal. We took a *taxicholo* (cycle rickshaw) to where the two decaying, rusting liners were moored on the lake.

The *Ollanta*, a 260 ft long, 2,000 ton vessel was built in Hull, England in the 1930s and had been transported in pieces by railway over the Andes and reassembled here in Puno. She was on a slipway out of the water, which still had a steam winch and steam cranes (both British built), and was a sight to behold. Once a luxurious cruise liner on the lake, she was being restored to her former glory.

The *Yavari*, which was moored nearby, was built by the James Watt foundry in Birmingham, England, in 1862 and is the world's oldest, single propeller driven, iron ship still in use. Unlike the *Ollanta*, this 140 ton ex-gunboat was transported in pieces over the Andes by mules, an amazing feat in itself. In 1952 Che and Alberto marvelled at the sight of these two ships, which seemed far too luxurious for the region. I myself marvelled at the ingenuity that got these massive ships here from England in the first place.

We loaded up the Nortons when we returned to the hostel. It was still very early and our plan was to make it to the ancient Incan city of Cusco, which was approximately 240 miles away. We were waved out of Puno by numerous white uniformed traffic policemen stood in their Inca Cola sponsored police boxes, blowing as hard as they could into their whistles and guiding the traffic out of the city.

We seemed to be climbing again and we passed through sun parched, mud brick villages. Smiling, waving children and the usual pack of growling dogs followed us through each one as we left the lake behind. The asphalt disappeared once again as the bumpy road gave way to dirt track and my bike weaved in and out of the huge potholes. The rain had ceased and it wasn't long before we dropped into a cauldron of activity, a town called Juliaca, which blew me away. Imagine about three thousand, three-wheeled bikes with the equivalent of a park bench strapped to the front, each carrying three passengers. Then add a two lane road which filters into one lane, add traffic lights every twenty yards and just for luck a few trucks, buses and cars all vying for a place and you get the picture! Sheer chaos, a free for all, but fun. Horns blaring and thick acrid smoke belching from the motorised vehicles all added to the furore which will live with me forever, partly because I am still alive to tell the tale!

We travelled steadily at 15,000 feet above sea level for miles. The snow-capped mountains made a picture postcard scene; the lush green valleys were full of llamas, cattle, pigs and local Quechua women working and tending the fields. The fast flowing rivers on either side of us cut through the land in torrents, which in a couple of hundred years would leave a plain of a thousand ox-bow lakes. The whole scene was so amazing that the Von Trapp family wouldn't have looked out of place had they come running down the mountainside singing *The hills are alive*. The scene was only interrupted by the sound of Pete's Norton backfiring as we passed through a tiny village called Agua Caliente, which was something we hadn't showered in for a long time!

Soon we were spiralling down to our Incan destination, the cascading river following our every twist and turn as the road unwound through the mountains. I was nearly knocked off *Kate* by a cow crossing the road and then by a dog, which having given up chasing Pete's bike hadn't realised I was following and very nearly brought both my journey and itself to an end. The land gave way on either side to red slashed mountains, with fields of crops on their sides at unimaginable angles. I was in awe at the sheer beauty of that place and just to remind us of where we were, every mud built house had an image of an Incan warrior painted on its walls, accompanied by the defiant words *Fuerte Inka*.

We stopped at a small shack *restaurante* at the side of the road but it didn't sell food, so after a bottle of Inca Cola we had to get on our way. It wasn't long before it started to rain again (as it tends to in the rainy season!) and the dry dust roads soon turned to thick brown mud, as we neared the province of Cusco. It was starting to get dark and thick black cloud was filling the sky. The asphalt road returned, albeit full of major potholes, and the torrent of brown rainwater made it seem like we were riding through a flowing river. We were in San Sebastian, a suburb of Cusco about two miles from the centre; the *Hostal* sign on the opposite side of the road dictated to us where we would be spending the night.

Chapter 12
The navel of the world

The room in the hostel was what I would describe as basic. It had two small single beds and a shower in the corner that looked like a torture device. (It had electric wires poking out of the shower head!) I poured the brown gravy-like water out of my boots and wrung my rain sodden combat trousers out in the sink. My clothing selection was now coming into question as it was a cold evening and my only dry clothes were a T-shirt and shorts. I had originally brought the combat trousers with me to wear when I wasn't riding the bike, but the weather over the last couple of weeks had been so hot that I couldn't wear my leather trousers, so I had worn my combats, which were now drenched in oil and sodden from the rainstorm.

We planned to go into the centre of Cusco for something to eat as San Sebastian was a very poor area. It was how I imagined Beirut to be during the Lebanese civil war. The majority of the side roads were just mud tracks, while the unkempt main road was lined with small workshops, hundreds of ironmongers and dilapidated housing.

We hailed a cab outside the hostel and headed for the Plaza de Armas, which is the main square in Cusco. The historic square is a beautifully landscaped plaza dominated by two Spanish churches and is a real hub of activity. There were a lot of people about, many of them tourists, spilling in and out of the many restaurants, cafés and small stores. I almost felt like I was on holiday.

We headed for the Norton Rat's Tavern, a bar named after the classic British motorcycles we were riding. It's a British/American style pub, and is a Mecca for locals, ex-pats and tourists. It is *the* place that all overland bike travellers head for in Peru, and we had read that nobody had ever turned up at the bar on a Norton motorcycle!

Jeff Powers the American proprietor of the bar is the proud owner of a 1974 Norton commando and has a real passion for British motorcycles, particularly the Norton brand. We were afforded a very warm welcome by Jeff and his lovely wife Yahira and we sat at the bar telling Jeff of our trip over a few beers. He was both fascinated and captivated by our journey and it wasn't long before Pete and Jeff got talking about the mechanical side of motorcycles and words like 'compression' and 'piston ring' were being passed back and forth. I was alone on this one; they may as well have been speaking in Klingon, as my knowledge of the combustion engine could be written on the face of a small postage stamp.

Thank God we were joined by a friend of Jeff's, an Australian guy called Glen Short, who was a part-time actor and published author. He had even done a stint in some Bollywood movies in India and was a very interesting character. As the beer and conversation flowed, the bar started filling up and the atmosphere was like that in any pub back home. For the first time since we had set out from Santiago in Chile, we were both relaxed and the hours just ticked away. It was past midnight when we finally got back to our downmarket suburban hostel in San Sebastian. We had burnt the candle at both ends!

I awoke the following day at about 6.30 a.m. It was Saturday, 14th February, and we enjoyed a breakfast of two dry bread rolls and a packet of nachos, washed down with a bottle of Inca Cola. Back in England I hoped my wife had received the roses I had pre-planned for delivery (yes girls, there are a few of us left out there!) for Valentine's Day.

My real priority that day though, was bike maintenance. My primary chain needed adjusting again and my side stand was no longer doing its job. It had started to crack where it was welded to the frame and with all the weight it was carrying, every time I put it on the stand, the Norton fell over on to its side. Pete's bike had worse problems. The electrics had failed, so we didn't even have one headlight between us and the problematic gearbox was shifting all over the place, as it had worked itself loose again.

Pete headed off to source a new battery and I adjusted the chain, added some oil and gave every nut and bolt a tweak as the roads here had vibrated a lot of them loose.

Next door to the hostel was what I would loosely describe as a maintenance workshop. It was an old tin shack with a crater in the ground that served as a pit for car maintenance. It looked like a hand grenade had been used to make the abyss and then the mechanics had simply dropped a couple of steel girders on some bricks and *voilà*, they had a ramp under which they could work!

I wheeled the Norton to the doorway of the workshop and the four mechanics came rushing towards me. They smiled as they looked at *Kate*, seeing the 60-year-old bike as something of a challenge. 'Soldadura?' I asked pointing at the crack on my side stand. 'Soldadura?' I repeated, as I liked the sound of the word. 'Si,' was the reply as they wheeled the bike into the workshop. The welding gear was dragged over the uneven soil floor to the bike and as the blue spark lit up the dark workshop, shouts of *Parada! Parada!* (Stop! Stop!) filled the air, along with the smell of petrol fumes. The young lad who was holding the bike had leant her over too far and petrol was flowing out of the tank. We were all very lucky that the spark hadn't ignited it.

The job was done and I paid the three sols (about 75 pence) requested, plus a tip of ten sols, as it felt shameful to pay only a pittance for a job which would have cost me several pounds back home. I wheeled the bike back to the hostel car park, where Pete was fitting a new battery to his bike and tightening up the gearbox with a new spanner he had bought. The bikes were fed, watered and ready for the next stage of our quest.

Che Guevara described Cusco as 'evocative'. Alberto Granado called the place 'wondrous'. I simply couldn't find a word to sum up that remarkable city, where the sands of past civilisations blow down the streets.

Cusco was the capital of the Inca Empire and it is said in Incan mythology that the place where a golden wedge dropped into the soil sank effortlessly was the place picked by the Incan gods for the chosen ones. Here they built a dominating city, surrounded by mountains and the fortress of Sacsayhuamán which was supposed to protect the palaces and temples of Cusco from its enemies. It was the Spanish conquistadores under the leadership of Francisco Pizarro, who conquered the city in 1534 and razed the temples and palaces to the ground. They used the Inca's stone foundations on which to build the Cathedral of San Domingo and the Church of La Compania in the Plaza de Armas to spread Christianity to the Andean world.

Subsequent earthquakes in the region caused major damage to both churches yet the foundations of the Temple of the Sun, on which they were standing, remained unscathed.

Even though the Spanish buildings dominate this magical city, you can't get away from the Incan influence, especially in the museums and libraries. I could write a whole book about this amazing place, and it took up more space in Che's diary than any other city on his journey.

We spent what was left of the day sightseeing around the city and even had a look round one of the museums that Glen had suggested to us. While exploring some of the shops selling Incan souvenirs we stumbled upon a tattooist's shop that specialised in Incan tattoos. Pete had toyed with the idea of getting a tattoo on this journey and this looked like a good opportunity to have the body art done. The tattooist invited us up into his studio, to show us his work. Tattooist, rather than tattoo artist, was definitely a better title for this young man and after looking at some of the photographs of his past victims, Pete quickly changed his mind. The majority of the Inca-style tattoos looked like they had been administered with a knitting needle using black boot polish instead of ink.

The following day (Sunday) we planned to visit the lost city of Machu Picchu. We had to book tickets for the trip through an agent, as it was inaccessible by road and the only way to get to it was walking, via the Inca trail, or by train.

'We would like to book a trip to Machu Picchu, tomorrow if possible,' Pete told the agent. No reply came, as the agent, resplendent in a beige safari suit, stroked his raven black goatee beard and stabbed an index finger onto the computer keyboard in front of him. Looking down at the screen and then staring right through Pete, he stroked the goatee once more.

'We would…' but before Pete could repeat the sentence, the agent answered the initial request.

'Two hundred,' he boomed.

'Sols?' Pete asked with optimism.

The agent allowed himself a broad smile.

'American dollars.'

'For both of us?' I chipped in.

'Two hundred American dollars each,' the broad smile had turned to laughter.

We were shocked and hadn't planned on the trip being so expensive. We looked at each other with a little uncertainty.

'It's expensive but we've come all this way and might never get another opportunity to see it,' Pete said.

'Is that your best price for two of us?' he asked.

The agent finally let go of his beard.

'If you pay by Visa, I will do the trip for one hundred and eighty dollars each, all inclusive.'

He had himself a deal and we handed our credit cards over.

'What is the address of your hotel?' he asked. 'The train leaves at 7 a.m. and the taxi will pick you up at 6.30 a.m.'

'It's a hostel in San Sebastian.' The smile disappeared and the agent looked horrified.

'San Sebastian? You are staying in San Sebastian?' he said, aghast.

We nodded in puzzled silence.

'No taxi will come to San Sebastian; you will have to make your way to San Pedro station where one of our agents will be waiting with your tickets and schedules. Be there for 6.30 a.m.'

Our credit cards were thrust back to us and we left the agent's office feeling like we'd been shafted.

We met up in Nortons with Jeff and Glen and I had what Jeff described as 'the best burger in South America'. I couldn't disagree with him, as I had mostly survived on chicken and chips over the last couple of weeks and he was an American after all.

Jeff was disappointed we hadn't turned up on the Nortons, but we had brought our maps of Peru so we could plan our onward journey. It wasn't long before the bar was filling up with fellow overland motorcycle travellers who wanted to exchange tales over a few dozen beers. We were joined by a couple of Germans, a Brazilian and an exceptionally tall guy from Alaska who all seemed to be making their trips on BMW R1150GSs after watching a TV series about a round the world motorcycle adventure!

From Alaska to Ushuaia (which is commonly regarded as the southernmost city in the world) was the common denominator of their travels and Jeff, our host, had even ridden his Norton from Cusco to Ushuaia, no mean feat in itself. The tales of their travels went on into the night helped by the never-ending rounds of drinks, but at around midnight we had to leave. We were due at San Pedro station at 6.30 a.m. and we didn't want to be late.

The brown mucilage they passed off as coffee at San Pedro station should have been served in slices it was so thick. It was only 6.15 a.m. and quite brisk, so the coffee helped to wake and warm me. We were waiting in the station café for the agent to meet us with our tickets and out of the window I could see the bright blue PeruRail backpacker train, its Pullman-style locomotive hooked up at the front and ready to go. I heard a shout of, 'Steve, Pete,' and looked round to see a pretty young girl waving tickets in our direction. We were handed the tickets as she explained the seating arrangements in the carriages and then told us that when we got to Machu Picchu station we had to, 'Look for Pedro Bandita waving a white flag!' The deafening screech of the train's horn filled the station, serving as a warning to get on board as the train was about to leave.

The train heaved itself out of the station and began to climb the steep mountainside out of Cusco. First it went forward and then reversed in a zig-zagging manner, pulling and pushing itself like a funicular up the sheer slope. At the top of the climb we were joined by a small, chocolate coloured river, which followed the trackside at every bend. The vegetation became tropical and lush and the cloud-kissed mountains on either side were covered in crops and greenery. Passing through small villages, the train let out loud rasps of its horn and the locals came up to the train trying to sell us their wares: cheeses, corn on the cob and freshly picked fruit. The four hour journey passed quickly. When we eventually entered the sacred valley, the small chocolate river had turned into a raging, white-water torrent that roared beside us. We then came to an abrupt halt and the train let out one more blast of its claxon. Perhaps it was a call to the Inca gods; it was so loud they would certainly have heard it. The horn was telling us we had arrived at Aguas Calientes, the closest station to Machu Picchu.

It was like getting off a ride at Disneyland, a mad rush that always ushers you through the gift shop. They sold everything from ponchos to fridge magnets, all adorned with the Machu Picchu name; every stallholder claimed to be a direct descendant of the Incas, and all accepted Mastercard!

Ahead of us there was a small Peruvian man waving a white flag, who looked like he had surrendered to the new wave of visitors heading his way. It was Pedro 'the Bandit' Bandita and believe it or not he didn't have a moustache or a Smith and Wesson. We were shown to a restaurant and issued with our entrance passes and bus tickets and then directed to our bus. I couldn't work out if our bus driver was a vice admiral in the navy or not, but he was wearing the uniform of one, in fact all the bus drivers were.

The bus climbed up the vertical mountainside which reached high into the sky and almost blocked out the daylight. The tropical jungle and fast flowing river made it an awesome sight, like the backdrop to *Raiders of the Lost Ark*, as we climbed higher and higher towards the entrance of the awe inspiring, spiritual, lost city of the Inca's, Machu Picchu.

Looking over the ruins from our vantage point, took our breath away. How anyone could have built or indeed wanted to build here was beyond belief. It was built around AD 1400 and was probably abandoned by the Incan rulers a century later at the time of the Spanish conquest. The Spanish conquistadores never found the city. Although known locally this remote place remained unknown to the outside world until it was 'discovered' by American historian, Hiram Bingham in 1911. It has withstood earthquakes and the test of time and is now classed as a heritage site in danger, mostly due to the high volume of tourists.

After our guided tour, we got back to the bus being driven by the vice admiral and headed back down the ravine road to the station. On the journey back, we sat on the other side of the train so we could take in the picturesque scenery we had missed on the way up, and after another serene four hour train journey, the train lowered us slowly down the dark mountainside and into the bright lights of Cusco. It had been a long day and the sightseeing had taken it out of us. After a couple of beers and one of Jeff's burgers, the conversation round the bar once more went on into the early hours, as we were joined by motorcyclists from far and wide. It had seemed a while since I had ridden *Kate* and in a funny way I was missing her. Jeff was desperate to see the Nortons and as he hadn't ridden his Commando for a while, we arranged for a ride round the city of Cusco the following day.

It was the first time I had ridden my Norton without the luggage attached and she handled like a dream as we weaved in and out of the traffic on our way towards the centre of the city. The throb of the engines echoed off the tight cobbled streets and heads turned in bewilderment as we passed. We arrived outside the Norton Rat's Tavern at about 1 p.m. and parked the bikes on the pavement, immediately drawing a crowd.

It wasn't long before Jeff pitched up on his Norton Commando and parked up next to us. The sight of the three Nortons drew a lot of attention and probably more photographs were taken of them that day than of the elaborate cathedral that threw its long shadow over us.

We were due to leave Cusco the following morning and Jeff wanted to show us the route out of the city. After three circuits of the square on the Nortons we followed Jeff up a side street and climbed the steep narrow road that led us to the outskirts of Cusco. The difference in the power of his twin cylinder engine (which gives out 60 horse power) was evident as Jeff left us standing in his wake, only slowing down when he realised he had three times the 'horses' we had! As we reached the city's outskirts, Jeff showed us the road we needed to take out of Cusco before we rode through the narrow streets once more, this time in line back down into the Plaza de Armas.

Mid-afternoon and we couldn't leave Cusco without visiting the Niños Foundation, a project that helps disadvantaged children. Jolanda van den Berg, the founder, was a Dutch tourist who first visited Peru in 1996. After seeing many children begging on the streets she decided to do something about it. She gave up her job and her home and leaving her family and friends behind in the Netherlands moved to Cusco where she immediately adopted two boys. After a year her adopted family had grown to 12 and she needed a bigger house!

Over the years Jolanda has opened two Niños Hotels and these help to finance the five children's centres she has opened, which provide hot meals, education, medical exams and dental visits to over 600 disadvantaged children daily, many of whom are orphans.

We met Jolanda at her hotel and she drove us to one of the children's centres. On arrival we were greeted by the staff and shown to a classroom where the children were drawing and painting. On entering, Jolanda was immediately mobbed by the children all shouting her name, and you could see the love and affection these children had for her. The scene was deeply moving and brought a lump to my throat. She showed us round the rest of the centre she has created, which has a theatre, a gymnasium and a garden where the children grow vegetables and keep rabbits.

On entering another classroom the children's chant of, 'Jolanda, Jolanda,' hit fever pitch and I was deeply moved as the children approached us, the *gringos*, and the boys shook our hands and the girls each gave us a kiss on the cheek. It was the most humbling experience of my life and something that will stay with me always. Looking at that slender Dutch girl, I could only admire what she has done and achieved there in Cusco for hundreds of children. Perhaps one day she will be 'Santa Jolanda'. It wouldn't surprise me.

We spent our last night in Cusco at our 'local', with Jeff and Glen. Our American host gave us two pearls of wisdom we should adhere to on our trip ahead: 'Don't ride at night in Peru, you will get robbed,' and, 'Plan your trip in hours, not miles, as the mountainous roads take time to ride.' It was good advice, yet tinged with a warning! Then the beer flowed once more and I had another of the 'best burgers in South America' as I knew it would be back to chicken and chips once we were back on the road.

I couldn't wait to climb on the Norton again; it had been nice to have a break, but nothing could beat the thrill of travelling across this vast continent on my *Kate*. We shook hands with everyone as we left the bar sometime around midnight. Jeff very generously picked up our tab and we waved goodbye to the many new friends we had made in this historic city.

Chapter 13
To infinity and beyond

I woke up on the morning of the 17th February in a very upbeat mood. The rain was beating against the window of our dismal room, but we were to continue on our journey and I was very excited at the thought of getting back on the Norton. I donned my waterproofs and we set off for our initial destination of Abancay, about three hours away. We fuelled up the bikes and filled our petrol cans on the higher 90 octane fuel instead of the usual 84, hoping it would help us when we were climbing the mountains. Then we rode across the main square of Cusco for the last time. The back end of my bike slipped violently from side to side as she struggled to grip the wet cobbled road, then the rain subsided and turned to drizzle and we steadily climbed the steep streets out of the city.

Passing through Anta we saw pigs and cows lining both sides of the road, which was sparsely covered with asphalt. Then, as is the custom in those parts, we were chased out of the village by the local canine gathering in hot pursuit of our bikes. The rain had stopped and the muddy road was drying out as the bikes slipped through numerous villages of mud built houses, where locals tended their livestock and waved and smiled as we passed. I could smell the lush green vegetation as the sun dried out and I smiled inwardly to myself at the tranquil land opening up before me. I could sense that it was going to be a good day.

We passed through Abancay around 11.30 a.m. and took the right fork in the road towards Ayacucho. The rain began again, and peppered my face hard, as we pressed on. The road had become difficult to ride as the mud ruts became deeper and forced the bike to go off the road on many occasions. Then, after riding about half an hour on very testing terrain a hand-painted sign warned us that the road ahead was closed due to *fango*, deep mud slides that had completely blocked the road. We had no alternative but to turn round and take the long way round to Lima via Nazca. Che and Alberto had taken the road to Ayacucho by truck; we simply had no choice on the Nortons. A sign reading, 'Camino Cerrado' (road closed), and a road barrier made up our minds for us!

We stopped for something to eat and a look at one of the Atlas maps Jeff had given us. The distance from Cusco to Nasca on the map looked about the same as the distance we had travelled from Puno to Cusco, so we hoped that was our destination.

The baked mud, part asphalt road had lots of little streams running across it which made the journey fun as my bike splashed through them. Then the road began to climb and climb and wind round the mountains in hairpin fashion. I was nearly wiped out by a coach coming in the opposite direction. The smell of its burning brakes took the sweet fragrance of the surrounding countryside away from my nostrils for several minutes and brought me back to reality. The road coiled like a corkscrew up the mountainside then back down the other side into a labyrinth of mountain roads. Many parts of the road were crossed by huge concrete cut outs which allowed the rushing water from the mountains to cross the road without washing it away and progress was very slow as the Nortons struggled up the mountains but performed heroically down them. After another map stop we realised there was no way we would make it to Nasca in a day, the small town of Puquio looked a more likely destination in the daylight hours that were left.

The rain subsided once more and the sun came out and brushed the mountainside in dazzling colours so we stopped to take our waterproofs off. At that moment a BMW motorcycle pulled up next to us. It was the tall Alaskan guy we had met in the Norton Tavern.

'Hi guys, where ya heading?'

'Puquio,' Pete replied.

'Do you mind if I ride with you? I'm heading there too.'

'We only average about 30 miles per hour on these bikes, but you're more than welcome.'

'How far is Puquio?' I asked.

'About 60 miles, I'll ride with you for a while.'

It was 3 p.m., and we hoped we'd be there in a couple of hours.

We started climbing another mountainside and the heavens just opened and absolutely lashed it down. There was no time to stop and put on our waterproofs and we were both instantly soaked to the skin. The guy from Alaska pulled up next to me clad in his all in one weatherproof suit and shouted above the din of my Norton, 'I'll see you guys in Puquio,' and with that he accelerated away from us like our bikes were stood still. Who could blame him? All we were doing was holding up his progress.

The sun came back once more and dried us out as we forged on into the mountainous region ahead. The terrain was becoming difficult as thick black clouds enveloped the snow capped mountains ahead and we donned our waterproofs once more and progressed slowly up the sierra. The road had become very narrow round the precipice and I just prayed that nothing would come the other way. To one side of the road was a man-made six foot deep gulley, which lined the mountainside to prevent the road from being washed away by the heavy rain. On the other side, sheer nothingness, canyons so deep they looked bottomless.

We went on and on hoping for a sighting of Puquio, climbing then descending the peaks, hoping to see the town in the distance round every bend. Then thick black cloud surrounded us and the torrential rain began again. We rode on into it as we had no choice, besides we couldn't be far away. It was 6 p.m., and even by our slow standards we should have covered the 60 miles in three hours.

Then a hammer blow came, a small sign at the roadside which read 'Puquio 98 km'. We stopped in a state of disbelief. 'Pete this is fucking serious, 98 kilometres, 98 kilometres,' I shrieked. I immediately blamed the Alaskan. 'He told us 60 miles three hours ago. Sixty fucking miles.'

Pete looked beside himself, horrified at our predicament. There was no town between us and Puquio, the sun was setting and we were stuck in the Andes with one headlight between us. We hadn't heeded Jeff's advice about time and distance, and riding in Peru at night and getting robbed was the least of our worries! As we looked over at the snow capped peaks ahead, the beauty had disappeared from them. They suddenly looked very dark and daunting and setting up the tents on the craggy mountainside was out of the question We had no choice but to carry on to Puquio.

The rain started to get heavier and I could feel the cold wetness in my groin as the waterproof trousers gave up being waterproof and allowed the rain in. My boots were slowly filling up in the monsoon-like conditions and my goggles started to steam up as the temperature dropped. I crouched down to try and keep warm and protect my eyes, which felt like they were having nails hammered into them as the rain came down relentlessly. I was getting cramp in my legs from being so tense and I could no longer feel my thighs as the freezing conditions penetrated my so-called waterproof trousers. My fingers were wrapped tightly around the handlebars, willing *Kate* up the mountain, but I could no longer feel them in my rain-sodden leather gloves.

As we peaked yet another mountain and the road levelled out a little, we could see ahead to another snow coated range. I was aghast that we were looking down over them. The rain had stopped and the Siberian temperatures were really beginning to bite and at that moment I just wanted to speak to my wife, my boys, anyone in the real world, to give me a means of escape. Then with darkness approaching fast I ran out of fuel and *Kate* came to a halt.

I dismounted and the ground felt like it was moving from side to side underneath me. Pete had stopped too as his bike also ran out of petrol a few yards ahead. With my freezing hands, I took my knife and cut my spare gallon can off the bungee that was holding it in place. I was shaking so much I don't know how much of the petrol I actually got into the fuel tank but I threw the can away and we carried on.

Darkness fell and with one headlight between us fear and panic started to grip me along with the cold. I started to pray, and then cursed the Peruvians for building their towns so far apart. 'Fuck, fuck, fuck, how much further,' I yelled out into the bitterly cold night air, not expecting any reply. I was scared and for that brief moment I just wanted my mum.

On we went sodden, freezing and totally demoralised. I couldn't feel my body and couldn't think straight, and then the sun was extinguished and with no stars above, we were pitched into total darkness, 4,500 metres above sea level. I had to stay as close to Pete as possible and follow his pale yellow headlight beam, as the tight road wound down the mountainside. But for one brief second I let him get too far in front and he disappeared out of sight, he was gone. I came to a stop, alone, in the darkness on that desolate mountainside. To my right was the six-foot deep, man-made ravine to catch the rainwater, but to my left was 'infinity and beyond' and certain death should I leave the road. I could see nothing in the darkness and I was on my own, scared and freezing.

Then I did the most stupid thing I have ever done in my life. Whether I was suffering from mild hypothermia and it was playing with my mind or just out of sheer desperation I started to ease the bike slowly down the mountain with my feet tapping at both sides. My mental state told me that if the slippery road disappeared from under my right foot I was over the six-foot deep, man-made gulley and if my left foot was thrust into space I was over the sheer drop off the mountain. I was like a blind man tapping a stick as tears ran down my face and I edged anxiously forward, in hope.

Then after what seemed like an eternity, I saw a light coming up the mountainside towards me, it was Pete. After realising he had lost me he had turned back and come to get. The relief I felt was immense. I started to follow him once more down the weaving mountain road, taking stupid risks to stay close to him; I was determined not to let him lose me again. I played a dangerous game trying to second guess which direction the next bend would take, while intermittently revving my engine loudly to let him know I was still close behind him as he couldn't see me in the ink-like night.

I prayed, cursed and shivered at the predicament we had got ourselves into, as the bends became sharper and more severe as we slowly progressed down the rugged mountainside. Then all of a sudden Pete went straight for a while and then his back wheel locked up and skidded across the gravel road.

'Shit, Shit what happened then,' I shouted at nobody in particular. Pete had come to an abrupt halt inches away from the sheer drop off the mountain; if he hadn't been able to stop it would have been certain death for both of us as I would certainly have followed him over. 'I was going too fast,' he said. 'We've got to get down off this mountain Steve, before we freeze to death.'

'Slow down Pete, just take it slowly, we'll get there,' I told him, more in hope than assurance. I had a feeling that we were looking at each other for strength to get us safely off the mountain that night, but inwardly I didn't think either of us believed we were going to make it.

I followed him once more as we progressed at about 10 mph in second gear, still holding my clutch in intermittently and revving my engine to let him know I was close behind. Ten miles per hour still seemed to be too fast under the circumstances, but neither of us wanted to perish on that mountain. Then disaster struck. On a very sharp left-hand bend Pete took his eye off the road for a split second to make sure I was behind him and didn't turn the bike. Bang! His Norton disappeared into the six foot man-made trench, throwing Pete forward into the mountain. If that bend had been the other way, it would have been certain death. Pete didn't move and I was in shock as I brought my motorcycle to a halt. The cold had sapped all my strength and I struggled to put my bike on its stand, but adrenalin took over and I went over to where Pete was slowly stirring as his headlight beam lit up the side of the channel so I could still see him. I felt like a helpless child and I wanted to cry but what help would that be?

'Pete, are you alright?' I shouted at him, but he didn't respond. 'Pete?'

'I'm alright, I'm alright,' he repeated several times as a surge of strength came over him and he climbed out of the crevice. 'I'm alright, I'm alright,' he kept saying while jumping around.

'You're not, alright,' I said to him. Blood was running down a deep cut to his cheek and his crash helmet had taken a battering. A chunk had been shaved off it where it had impacted against the mountainside, but thankfully it had done its job. I still didn't think he was alright. He was walking around like somebody had jump-started him with defibrillators, still claiming, 'I'm alright, I'm alright.'

We both stopped and looked at each other; what could we do now? We hadn't seen another vehicle in hours and I couldn't ride on to get help, as I had no headlight on my bike and Pete's bike was rammed tight into that deep ditch, its headlight still shining into the nothingness. We tried in vain to lift the bike out, but we had no chance. We were too cold, too wet and too demoralised. Even at full strength in the light of day, we wouldn't have been able to get *Caca* out of that deep ditch on our own.

Then in the distance we saw headlights coming down the mountain. As they got closer I stood in the road to flag the vehicle down, it was an overland coach, but the driver had no intention of stopping. He nearly took me out as he hurtled past us at speed, perhaps thinking we were robbers! Our hopes faded and I shouted numerous obscenities as the coach faded into the distance. Stupid plans entered our heads; we weren't thinking straight and quite honestly didn't know how to get out of the predicament we were in. Shouting atrocities and vulgarities at the mountains and surrounding environment wasn't solving our problem, but we had to get off that mountain or succumb to it.

Then after a while another set of headlights appeared, coming up the mountain. I could see it was a pick-up truck; it passed us slowly, weighed up the situation then reversed to where we were. He spoke out in Spanish but we didn't understand him. We must have looked like two lost waifs standing at the side of the road, wet and shivering.

'We need help,' I said. I think the giant of a man who climbed out of the truck wearing T-shirt and shorts could see that for himself.

'Where are you from?' he spoke perfect English.

'England.'

'I have been to England?'

'Whereabouts?' I asked striking up a somewhat bizarre conversation and expecting the usual reply of 'London'.

'Ipswich, I worked there for a few years. Great place, great people.' The conversation was surreal.

He looked at the bike and jumped down into the ditch next to it, we followed but still the three of us couldn't lift the bike out. A bitter wind crossed the mountain and it started to rain again, quickly turning into hail. There were more lights coming towards us and as a lorry got near to us the big guy 'from Ipswich' whistled, and then shouted loudly at the truck demanding it to stop. The driver got out and came over, but even with the four of us we hadn't a chance of lifting the bike out.

'I will use the winch,' the truck driver said and with that he manoeuvred his truck at an angle, completely blocked the road, and hitched up the winch to the bike. We lifted and he wound the winch in gently. All feeling had gone in my body, I was numb and couldn't muster any strength to help lift the bike, but thankfully the winch did most of the work. The bike was dragged to the side of the road with very little damage apart from a broken foot peg. We shook hands with them both, 'Muchas gracias, muchas gracias,' we repeated. Then in a blink, they were gone. The story of the Good Samaritan entered my head – the pick-up guy was certainly one of those. I just hoped the people of Ipswich had shown him the same thoughtfulness and generosity he had afforded us.

Back to reality and we were still on the mountainside in total darkness, torrential rain and with a few miles to go before we got to Puquio. We got back on our bikes and literally rode at a snail's pace as we carried on down the mountain. After about half an hour we saw lights ahead, it had to be Puquio.

The road turned to thick mud as we entered a street with houses on it. I was confused as to where we were. Puquio had looked like a main town on the Atlas map Jeff had given us and this place certainly wasn't a big town. I saw a lady ahead and shouted to her in my limited Spanish, 'Centro, centro?' She pointed straight down the street and disappeared into one of the small houses. We followed the street which seemed to be leading us nowhere as the small row of houses we had passed disappeared into the distance behind us. Then out of nowhere a tuk-tuk appeared, struggling through the mud and swaying from side to side to try to get traction. I flagged it down, and asked the driver, 'Centro, centro?'

'Plaza de Armas?' he said thrusting his finger in the direction from which he had come, and then carried on with his fare.

Pete was struggling riding without his foot peg and I was still unsure whether he was suffering from concussion from the crash. We stopped for a moment, to take stock and gather our thoughts. We didn't know where we were or what time it was. Then the tuk-tuk driver we had seen a few moments before pulled up behind us.

'Plaza de Armas, hotel, hotel!' he shouted and waved at us to follow him. We followed him closely down the mud-bath weaving to avoid the huge craters and manholes that were consistently in our path. Eventually we came to a street and civilisation! He pointed us down the street and in an instant he had disappeared into the night.

Hostal Maverick, the neon sign read, first flashing on in red then flashing blue. I climbed the steep, narrow stairs to the desk that served as reception. The young boy behind the desk took a long look at me, then laughed. I looked down at the puddle of water that had gathered beneath my muddy boots and at my combats caked in mud and laughed with him; I was relieved we had made it here, relieved to be alive. We were safe; we had made it to Puquio!

'Do you want to see the room?' he broke the silence.

'No, no, we'll take it. Does it have hot water?'

'Si, si, agua caliente.'

We parked the bikes in a yard about four blocks away and covered them with a huge plastic sheet. The young lad carried our bags on his head and showed us to our room. Pete and I just looked at each other, we were both very emotional, but we had come through the danger and survived. It had taken us five and a half hours to cover the last 60 miles. We had been taught a valuable lesson: distance in Peru is in hours, not miles. We should have listened to Jeff!

The following morning as I stared in a trance-like state at my pile of wet clothes on the floor, I was still shivering. I took a hot shower to try to thaw myself out. I stared out across the rooftops at the blue sky; it was like being in a different world, away from the threat of last night's events. In fact it was almost as if last night hadn't happened, such was the tranquillity of the day. I donned my leather trousers and put some plastic bags into my soggy boots and put them on. I hoped they would dry out in the sun as we went to look for somewhere to have breakfast. With Pete wearing his leather trousers as well, we looked like a couple of members of the Village People walking down the muddy street as we left the hostel.

Puquio, looked like it hadn't changed in centuries. Open drains lined the muddy streets which gave way to a square (Plaza de Armas) with a beautiful pink church. The surrounding roads were filled with locals selling an array of fruit and vegetables which added a blend of bright yellows, greens, oranges and purples to the dull backdrop of the mud-baked housing. Live pigs and sheep were on sale and guinea pigs in wooden boxes were on a 'buy one, get one free' offer (presumably because one wouldn't satisfy your appetite at dinner). A variety of caged birds squawked loudly above the din of the market traders, shouting out their offers to the passing locals. To add to the commotion the odd tuk-tuk taxi tried to weave in and out of the stalls, where there was very little chance of getting through, honking their horns in anger and adding to the whole anarchy of the market. The curtain on the scene was brought down when the sun overhead was blocked out by a condor soaring high above. Its ten-foot wingspan stretched to the maximum as it circled above and brought the town to a standstill as everyone looked up at the mythic bird in reverence. Then it disappeared out of sight and the volume was turned back up and the chaos continued.

After breakfast we went to the yard where the bikes were parked to assess the damage to Pete's Norton. Along with a broken foot peg, the drop into the gulley the night before had bent the kick-start right into the bike and would need repairing, but apart from that he had been incredibly lucky. After a visit to the town welding shop we loaded up the bikes. I packed my wet clothes into a plastic bag and we set off on our way, heading for the town of Nazca.

Chapter 14
Forth by day

As we left the PetroPeru gas station the teeming rain started again. The road out of Puquio was worse than any we had encountered on the journey so far and made our bad road in Argentina seem like an *autopista*. I don't know how the Peruvians get away with putting it on a map and calling it a road but the bikes were getting shaken up badly once again. My concentration levels had to be at their highest as I did my best at riding in-between the divots and ruts that made up the hard dirt trail that was slowly turning to mud under the torrential rainfall. My Norton bottomed out on several occasions as it proved impossible to avoid the potholes. It should have carried a government heath warning – it was a very dangerous trail to ride!

We slowly progressed back up into the mountains and the bikes took a real pounding. Ahead of me I could see Pete's sleeping bag was trailing on the ground behind him, but I couldn't catch up to him due to the state of the road surface and when we eventually stopped, most of it had chafed away. I also found that I'd lost all my wet clothes that had been tied to the back of my bike in a plastic bag, but we had travelled too far to go back and look for them. The track was terrible and it came as a shock when I saw a sign for road works (all the way to Nazca). Perhaps there would be an improvement ahead. I was optimistic as we passed intermittent gangs of road workers.

Fallen rocks littered the road as we weaved on towards our destination. The road was rough but the scenery was magnificent, awe inspiring, the best yet, and we stopped to admire the view. I felt like I was on top of the world, like I could reach up and touch God's soul. I took a deep breath and then we dropped down the spiralling road and went from 4,200 metres on an ear-popping ride to just under 600 metres in a few miles. It was a breathtaking ride with a backdrop to match and, as we entered Nazca, the sun was shining and I had a Peruvian smile on my face.

We headed for the Plaza de Armas where we got a hostel room. Then we went into the centre of the town that, less then 15 years ago, had been completely wiped out by an earthquake. The multicoloured, double storey houses all with columns, stood round the beautifully manicured gardens that filled the Plaza de Armas. Nazca was a beautiful town and my first job there was to buy some new clothes to replace the ones I had lost.

'London fashion,' the sales assistant shouted at me through the curtain that covered the changing room door. 'Peru fashion,' I replied as I looked down at the cotton combat trousers I was trying on for size. The trousers went to just below my knees and when I walked out of the changing room the two women in the shop burst into laughter. 'I need longer trousers and smaller waist,' I gesticulated using sign language and raised my voice in the hope they would understand me. The giggles stifled as I stood there in the shop, looking ridiculous. 'London Fashion,' the assistant repeated before howling in laughter again and handing me a pair that would have fitted a beanstalk dweller with a fifty inch waist. 'No, no, my size.'

I decided to take a look on the rack myself. I picked up an olive pair of trousers with side pockets and took them into the changing room, and hastily closed the curtain behind me. They were too big round the waist but were the nearest fit I was likely to get, with the two cackling assistants who were trying to serve me. 'London fashion,' I said and picked up a T-shirt that matched. 'London fashion,' she replied as she gave me my change and handed the plastic bag to me.

I looked back at the shop as I walked down the street. The two assistants were waving at me through the dirty shop window. Above them a brightly lit sign in big white letters read 'LONDON FASHION' with a dodgy image of a clock that was supposed to resemble Big Ben making up the 'I' in fashion!

We left Nazca early on the morning of 19th February in the hope that we could make the capital, Lima by 6 p.m. The road was good asphalt which mirrored in the bright sunlight ahead. We entered dry arid land with the Andes far away to our right. We could have almost been back riding in the Atacama Desert as the temperature was so stifling. The windless plateau we were riding across was only broken up by tall wooden viewing towers that were all over the flat sands. We were passing the famous Nazca Lines, a series of ancient geoglyphs in the desert which can only be seen from the wooden towers or by aircraft as some are over 200 metres (660 ft) across. They are of some sort of religious significance and are many thousands of years old. The hundreds of lines all over the desert depict hummingbirds, spiders, monkeys, sharks and many other species and shapes which must have taken one hell of a lot of planning by the ancient Nazca culture.

We passed through flourishing green valleys as we rode through the villages Llipata and Santa Cruz and refuelled just outside Ica. We made good time and the bikes were going well at the low altitude as we proceeded through the sparse pampas towards Guadalupe and beyond. I took the lead and ahead I could see what looked like a sea mist or low cloud which blanketed the whole horizon. The side wind was by now very boisterous and blowing violently from the west, whipping up mini twisters in the sand. Then suddenly we were engulfed and I realised we had ridden into a sandstorm. For a few moments I thought everything was okay, but then someone opened up the *Book of the Dead* and unleashed hell! The wind roared and I couldn't breathe as the sand filled my mouth and nostrils and we rode on, hoping we would get through it. As visibility got worse and the sand and intense heat choked me I gasped for every breath and it became unbearable. I was nearly blown off the bike and I couldn't see a thing through my riding goggles, but foolishly I carried on, half expecting a plague of locusts to follow the turbulent dust storm that had deluged us. I stopped and tried to look back into the obscure brown dust that had overcome us and gasped for air as the sweat poured off me in the intense oven-like temperatures. I could see nothing; the road behind me had disappeared behind the sand and there was no sign of Pete.

I turned round and rode back trying to make out the road, as the severe winds continued to whip up the sand and cover everything in its path. I rode about half a mile back before I saw the outline of Pete's bike parked up, but no sign of Pete. I parked up next to his Norton and in the distance I could barely make out the outline of Pete trying to take shelter under a small bush, his slight frame in the foetal position already half covered where the vicious wind had blown sand up against him. I could hardly hear him shout out to me as the wind howled around us and the sand sugared my face.

'Why did you carry on into the sand?' he shouted

'I didn't realise what it was, I thought we would get through it,' I hollered back.

'My bike just stopped, there must be sand everywhere,' he tried to explain, but the sentence disappeared into the relentless wind.

I lay next to him under the small bush that danced in the continuous gale and prayed that it would soon be over. But after two hours under the baking heat the onslaught seemed to be getting worse. We had hardly exchanged a word as the sand clogged up my mouth and suffocated the air out of my lungs but a decision had to be made before we succumbed to the elements. 'Pete, we've got to get out of here, this could go on for days,' but it was difficult to speak as the sand entered my lips. 'We'll leave the bikes and try to hitch a lift,' I added.

Pete had realised the danger we were in and was in total agreement that the only way out of our predicament was to 'abandon ship' and leave the Nortons behind. An executive decision had been made by us both and we chained the bikes together, got our luggage and crossed the road in the hope that someone would come along and get us the hell out of there to safety. Over an hour passed and our hopes were beginning to wane as our water supply got low and the sandstorm showed no sign of letting up. Then we saw headlights approaching and after waving like a couple of castaways stranded on a desert island, Pete suddenly jumped into the road and brought the approaching vehicle to an immediate halt.

The Jeep's air conditioning was cool and soothing and it was great to be able to breathe, without covering my face to avoid the sand entering my nostrils. Ica was some 45 miles back in the direction from which we had come, and the couple who picked us up were thankfully heading there. The driver and his wife were slightly bemused at finding two *extranjeros* at the side of the road and thought we were slightly crazy to be riding in such conditions. They dropped us off at the central bus station in Ica, where the remnants of the sandstorm still filled the air.

I left Pete at the side of the road in a very emotional state and went to look for somewhere to stay. I looked back for a brief moment to see if he was okay. He looked forlorn and despairing sat there on the pavement with our bags and I could see the last few hours had really affected him.

I entered the bus station which had a hostel and looked at my reflection in the mirror behind the young receptionist. She stared at me in bewilderment as I looked like I had taken part in Operation Desert Storm. There was sand all over me, even outlining where my goggles had been on my face.

I was first into the shower as I allowed Pete a moment alone to gather his thoughts. I had a strange calmness about me, even though we had come close to not surviving the dust storm, but Pete was clearly still quite shaken by the whole episode and I genuinely felt for him. He told me later that as he lay there in the sand, he had thought of his wife and children and had an overwhelming urge to write a farewell letter to them. That is how close he felt we were to not getting out of there!

Once we were showered and changed we got our heads together and decided we had to recover the bikes immediately. We took a tuk-tuk to a Yamaha shop we had seen on the way into Ica, to ask if they had a recovery vehicle. We met a young man there called Alejandro Omas Serna Brava who owned a Velorex (Chinese motorcycle) dealership who offered to help us hire a truck. We climbed on the back of his Velorex which had a tipper body and set off into the hysteria that is the Peruvian roads.

He drove us round for a while, horns blaring from all directions, before spotting a rather motley crew who had a plot with trucks for sale. Every truck on the plot had shiny hub caps and reminded me of the fairground trucks back home. Come to think of it, the guy Alejandro spoke to resembled a bare knuckle gypsy fighter and with his pugilistic nose, he looked like he had won a lot of second prizes! 'Too much, too much,' Alejandro muttered to himself as he jumped back on the scooter and without explaining anything, whizzed back round into the loony tune traffic system.

We pulled up at a building which was half breeze block and half tent. 'Wanxing' (yes I laughed too) the banner proclaimed in three foot high letters on the breeze block walls to the entrance of the building. It was a dealership for another make of Chinese motorcycle owned by Alejandro's brother, Gustavo. We explained in broken Spanish about what had happened and where the bikes were. One hundred and fifty sols (about £30) was the reply and we had a deal to recover the 'girls'.

Gustavo threw the keys to his Nissan pick-up at me and indicated to me that he wanted me to drive. The cab crew of the pick-up took up most of the vehicle and it was very debatable whether the bikes would fit on the back of the flatbed. There was only one way to find out, as I navigated my way through the bustling traffic and burst out of Ica to the relative tranquillity of the highway on which we had left our bikes. Conversation was very limited on the journey as the Nissan's stereo system was at full torque, blasting out South America's answer to rave music, while the two brothers somehow managed to chat away on their mobile phones and I drove on into the wilderness.

The sandstorm had lapsed as we drove on towards the bikes with the wind just spreading smatterings of sand across the road in front of us. The drive was very bleak and we were still deflated from the incident that had caused us to abandon the bikes only three or four hours earlier. Then, up ahead in the distance, we could see people milling around the Nortons. My first thought was that we were being robbed but as we neared the crowd I could clearly make out the word *Policia*. There were two police pick-up trucks, four policemen and three highway workers with shovels clad in high visibility orange who were shovelling the sand dune that had built up next to the bikes. There was also a reporter from the local newspaper, who fired dozens of questions at us as soon as we got out of Gustavo's pick-up truck. We told him what had happened, with Pete explaining that, 'due to the age of the Nortons they had no air filters to protect them from the sand'. After the press reporter had written down our story and the police officers had each had their photograph taken with the bikes, they helped us to lift the Nortons onto the flatbed of the pick-up truck. Then with the now customary smiles and numerous handshakes we left them and I spun the truck round in the road and headed back to Ica.

We arrived at Alejandro's bike shop where we unloaded the bikes, shared a couple of beers and arranged to meet up the following morning. After a supper of chicken and chips we headed to our hostel for a sleepless night as my mind mulled over the day's events. Pete told me he almost wished the bikes had been stolen to put an end to the nightmare, but thankfully we had got them back and we were all safe.

On reaching Alejandro's bike shop the next morning at 9 a.m. Pete immediately stripped his carburettor down and got to work removing the sand with an air line Alejandro had set up. Gustavo arrived shortly afterwards and threw the pick-up's keys at me. 'My older brother's bike has broken down and needs to be picked up, will you drive me there?' How could I refuse? I left Pete to sort out the Nortons and set off with Gustavo to recover the stricken bike.

Gustavo was a cheery lad, who was always smiling and was immaculately dressed with perfectly coiffured hair. The only thing that seemed to let him down was the fact that he couldn't drive! As he explained to me on the way, 'I saw the pick-up and had to buy it. I will learn to drive soon.' To him it was a status symbol, and I was certainly handy when it came to recovering motorcycles.

I followed the road Gustavo directed me down which would have been inaccessible to most vehicles, except 4x4s, trail bikes and Nortons! It was horrendous and the pick-up truck seemed to make harder work of it than the Nortons would have done. We recovered his brother's trail bike which had a buckled wheel and dropped it off at his bike shop to be repaired. Then Gustavo summoned his mechanic to come with us and we set off to another breakdown. After an hour's drive into the countryside we arrived at a big old farmhouse that was painted brilliant white to reflect the sun. It had the perfect air conditioning system – windows without any glass in them!

The farmer had purchased a brand new pick-up trike from Gustavo and with only 37 km on the clock the lights had failed. While the mechanic messed with the electrics on the bike Gustavo tried to convince the farmer that it was a minor fault while I sat in the living room with the elder of the family watching Schalke versus Borussia Dortmund on his old black and white TV! There were four generations of the same family all living under one roof. Eventually the *Madre* of the family came in to me and held out a jar of water and some green sprigs. She ushered me away from the Bundesliga game I was watching, towards the three-wheeled Wanxing that was now proudly showing off its headlights to the accompaniment of its flashing indicators.

I was a little bewildered as to what was going on, then a smiling Gustavo explained, 'She would like the gringo to bless the bike for good luck,' and he intimated for me to put the green sprigs into the jar of water and splash it over the trike. I did as I was instructed and 'blessed' it! Then we all celebrated with hugs, cheek kisses and a glass of cold orange juice.

When I arrived back at Alejandro's bike shop I found a note from Pete saying that he wasn't feeling very well and had gone back to the hostel to lie down for a while. My bike had been cleaned and all there was left to do was spray the new primary chain that had been fitted and pack my stuff. I arranged to meet Alejandro and Gustavo at the shop that night at about 8 p.m. and then I went to grab some food at the Pollo Grill.

We knocked loudly on the wooden door of the Wanxing dealership which was promptly opened by Gustavo who looked immaculate in a white, crisp, well-ironed shirt which was draped over a handgun that was tucked down the side of his navy blue Farah-style trousers. His hair was impeccable and didn't move in the slight evening breeze as the thick coating of hair lacquer did its job.

'Hola, come in.' He beckoned us into the garage to where his smartly dressed mechanic, his brother and a friend who was a money lender were drinking beer out of plastic cups. We were offered a drink which I gratefully accepted but Pete, who was still feeling unwell, declined. We were going to head out to a club called Barena, which was on the outskirts of Ica and I suddenly felt underdressed in my oversized 'London Fashion' combat trousers. Pete didn't look at all well and as the beer continued to flow he made his apologies and left to go back to the hostel to lie down.

We were in high spirits as the motorised Velorex scooter taxi arrived at about 10.30 p.m. to take us to the club and despite the language barrier we got on brilliantly. The journey took us through one of the roughest areas I have ever been through, but then out of nowhere the bright neon lights of Barena appeared like an oasis and the sound of Cuban derived salsa music filled the air. It was a really cool place and we had to squeeze past dozens of people who had formed a huge conga line to get served at the bar.

We stood at the bar ordering rounds of drinks as cavorting couples danced shamelessly behind us on the dance floor to the seductive clave rhythm with fire in their souls and their feet. The whole place meandered from side to side in one massive Latin American carnival charanga to the brass sounds coming from the huge overhead speakers and I suddenly wished I could dance the salsa. I looked at Gustavo as he sat at the bar, the wooden grip of his pistol protruding from his belt in a show of defiance. Then I looked around at the money lender behind me, he too had what looked like a revolver sticking out of his waistband, in fact every guy in there except me and Alejandro seemed to be packing a piece! A leggy blonde came over smiling at the money lender and whispered in his ear and he let out a raucous laugh. Flirting with each other, I imagined the conversation to be along the lines of, 'Is that a pistol in your pocket or are you just pleased to see me?' Then he pushed her onto the dance floor and his hands risked a serious repetitive strain injury as they clenched her gravitating buttocks to the salsa beat.

I ordered another five bottles of Cusquena as across the bar a small, dark skinned man gave me a smile that was menacing and lingered a little too long. I looked away then took another look back as I picked up the bottles but he was still staring at me with a sneer.

'Gustavo, I think it is about to kick off,' I said pointing discreetly over to the guy who was by now looking rather confrontational. 'Don't worry Steve,' he said, drunkenly patting his gun. 'You are protected.' That's what I was worried about: the fact that the place might turn into Tombstone, Arizona and the gunfight at the OK Corral.

'Gustavo, I think we should leave,' I pleaded. 'You worry too much Steve,' and with that he waved his hand over towards the front entrance of the club. A small stocky man with a big chin came over to Gustavo and asked what was wrong.

After a lot of pointing and a few words to each other the small man went over to the other side of the bar and had words with the guy who had taken an instant dislike to me. He returned, pulling back his shirt to reveal a .44 Magnum revolver, to say, 'Gringo, don't worry, you are protected.' I looked over to the other side of the bar and the sneering man was nowhere to be seen.

The money lender staggered back over to our group and reached over for his beer.

'Steve you like the music? Have a dance,' and he beckoned the leggy blonde over to us. I shimmied from side to side like an aged uncle at a wedding, while the leggy blonde was shaking her booty with so much seismic energy it would have measured on the Richter scale. I suddenly felt about 143 years old, and while Elvis had sung the words 'If you can't find a partner use a wooden chair,' this girl had found the tree from which it had been carved. It was time for me to leave.

I was awoken the following morning by a high pitched voice hollering through a megaphone. I got out of my sand-filled bed to take a look at what all the commotion was about. Outside there was a girl on a three-wheeled bike selling bread! Pete was still feeling ill, but we had to leave for Lima and we left the hostel room and got a taxi to Alejandro's bike shop.

The shop was locked up when we arrived and after banging loudly on the door for over ten minutes, Alejandro appeared with a towel wrapped round him, hungover and smiling. 'It was a good night Steve,' he said pulling back the big wooden door to let us get our bikes. 'Perhaps you should learn the salsa,' he taunted, as I wheeled *Kate* out into the beautiful morning sunshine. I gave him a hug and climbed on my bike as he and his staff waved us off. Ica had been an unexpected stopover, but a memorable one.

Chapter 15
The world's highest city?

As we passed the place we had abandoned the bikes, it was hard to imagine that less than 48 hours earlier a massive dust storm had halted our progress. The only signs of the storm were one or two council workers we passed shovelling small sand dunes off the road as the sun beat down on the tranquil road to Guadalupe. It was a beautiful day and the ride was more than pleasurable as we headed out towards the Pacific coast, with only the stench of burning rubbish marring the spectacle before us. The Peruvians seem to tip all their rubbish at the roadside and simply set fire to it and to my mind they were destroying a beautiful part of their country. *Kate* was performing very well after the overhaul she had been given and the engine was crooning beautifully as we dropped down towards the Pisco valley.

A smell like pea pods filled my nostrils as we passed field after field of grapevines, which stretched for miles as we rode the coast road to Chincha Alta. A cold sea mist suddenly wrapped itself around us, but was quickly dispersed as the sun peaked, to reveal the undulating white waves of the Pacific breaking on the golden sands of the Peruvian coastline.

The amber beach was undisturbed and idyllic, just like the pictures you see in travel brochures, but a few miles further up the coast towards Jaguay, the halcyon landscape was intruded upon by thousands of open battery chicken sheds on the beach. The sheds were over 100 foot long and over 40 foot wide and contained

millions of birds which were packed in cages and baking
in the 30 degree heat. We rode for a few miles towards
San Vicente de Canete before leaving the disturbing
scene which I called 'chicken beach' behind. I made a
mental note not to eat chicken in that region.

On and on we rode passing through Lapa Lapa and
Calango before we entered Lima, the capital and largest
city in Peru. Lima is the third largest city in Latin
America with a population of over eight and a half
million people and accounts for more than two thirds
of Peru's industrial production, and you could tell that
by the amount of traffic we had to dodge on the way
to the centre. The single track road we had been riding
suddenly exploded into a five lane highway and we
were swamped by cars, trucks and buses, all belching
out a polluting fog of black acrid fumes.

We hadn't a clue where we were going, but decided to
get off the highway as soon as possible, before one of us
was taken out by the absurd driving that was going on
all around us. We took a slip road which led us off the
main highway and we followed a sign for 'Sur Avenue'
that led us to the very affluent district of San Borja.

San Borja is a suburb of Lima that was planned
and developed from the beginning in an orderly
fashion. Surrounded by beautiful parks and gardens,
a Hollywood-style sign in large white letters proudly
spells out the name of the district. The streets in the area
we were in were all named after famous painters and
philosophers and San Borja is also the home of Peru's
Museo de la Nacion (Museum of the Nation) and the
Biblioteca Nacional (The National Library) which were
both visited by Che and Alberto, although back in 1952
they were in the centre of Lima.

We pulled up at a petrol garage to refuel and while
Pete looked after the bikes I set off to look for a hotel

or hostel. I tried every place on the main road and was rebuffed by them all. It turned out that for the middle and upper classes of Lima, San Borja was the place to go to at weekends, and some hotels cost as much as 300 sols (about £60), which was well out of our price range anyway! I eventually found a cheap hostel which had the unusual practice of renting rooms out by the hour, and after a little bartering, which involved safe parking in the yard for the bikes, we had beds for the night. The room had no windows and was very small but it did have the bonus of having a TV.

As I lay on my bed I flicked on the TV, but it only had one channel, which was showing a writhing couple shouting out in German. I turned the TV off, but could still hear the romping couple up to their shenanigans as the whole hostel had the same channel on and it echoed down the corridor filling the warm night air. Then it slowly dawned on me, rooms by the hour? One porn channel? We had booked ourselves into a knocking shop!

We woke on a sunny Sunday morning and checked out very early to some rather funny looks from the young receptionist on the desk. The place was deserted and we loaded up the bikes with our luggage. We would shortly be back on track and once again following the trail of Che and Alberto. There was one small problem though. The security guard who had the key to the large metal sliding doors of the yard in which we had parked our bikes couldn't be contacted. The only other key to the huge padlock was held by the manager and it would be a few hours before he came into the hostel. Using my initiative, I quickly found a 'key' that would fit the giant padlock in the shape of a pickaxe that I used to prise open the lock, much to the bemusement of the remonstrating receptionist. I slid the huge steel doors open and we rode out and joined the throng of beeping cars heading out of Lima.

As we scaled the road out of the city, the smog that covered the mountains we were about to ascend took on the dark haze you would associate with London in the 'Jack the Ripper' years. We climbed the steep road through the villages of Matucana and San Mateo, again being chased by packs of dogs and passing lots of huge rockfalls which had thankfully been cleared by heavy machinery that had been drafted in during the rainy season. *Kate* and *Caca* seemed to have taken on a new lease of life after the repairs Pete had given them in Ica and they rose to the challenge presented to them like Sir Edmund Hillary tackling Everest.

Our destination was Cerro de Pasco, a mining town high up in the Andes and one of the highest cities in the world. We passed the Junin plains at some 3,500 metres above sea level where, back in 1824, a historical precedence was set when Argentinian, Chilean, Peruvian and Venezuelan troops fought shoulder to shoulder to defeat the Spanish in the war for independence. The dark clouds came down to meet us as we climbed higher and higher into the grey wilderness and I wondered to myself how the conquistadores had put up with the biting cold.

We passed herds of alpacas and llamas grazing on the barren hinterland as a light rain started to inhibit what was left of the daylight, making even the grass in the forbidding scrubland look grey. The light rain quickly turned to hail as the freezing cold bit deep once again. I was nearly wiped out by yet another oncoming coach that was driving on the wrong side of the road and had failed to see me in the prevailing cloud that had now wrapped itself round the mountainside. Then suddenly the rain stopped and I was plunged into sheer darkness as we entered a tunnel that had been cut through the mountainside. The lack of a headlamp on my bike now causing me real peril, I rode on blindly through the darkness, trying to stay close to Pete's Norton in front of me.

We eventually reached a fork in the road and took the left track to Pasco. The hail had ceased and although I was bitterly cold this was forgotten as I had to concentrate hard and navigate *Kate* down the shale track while trying, at all costs, to avoid the huge potholes and uncovered manholes in the makeshift road.

Pasco is in Peru's most famous mining area. Lead, zinc and silver are all extracted and as Alberto and Che commented at the time of their visit, 'The mines are in Yankee hands.' It was a depressing place, and the locals looked gaunt and miserable with no sign of the famous Peruvian smile. The bland grey buildings merged into the bleakness of the dreary damp night air as we rode down into the town looking for somewhere to stay. Then suddenly my bike disappeared from under me, as the rear wheel dropped into a huge grate that was in place across the road to stop the rainwater from flooding the city centre.

I was surrounded by locals who found my predicament rather amusing and helped me to lift the bike out of the huge cattle grid. I'd brought smiles to a few faces, if only for a brief moment.

Hostal Wong was the only place in town with safe parking for the bikes and the welcome we got from the woman who owned it was the only warmth we found in Cerro de Pasco as the temperatures continued to plummet. It was bitterly cold and with no hot water in the rooms and unable to shower, we dropped our bags and went to the nearest café for something to eat. We placed our order in broken Spanish, each chipping in with a few words, and then waited to see what we would be served! A bowl of chicken and rice soup, chicken and chips and a bottle of Inca Cola to wash it down with, all for five sols (about £1) was the impressive result! And I didn't care whether it had come from 'chicken beach' or not, I was starving!

We got back to the hostel at about 8.30 p.m. and decided to go to bed as there was nothing else to do. The temperature in my room had dropped below freezing and although there were a few heavy blankets on the bed I decided to put my sleeping bag inside the blankets and sleep fully clothed to try and get my body temperature back up to normal. I was shivering and my nose and lips were a funny blue colour as I climbed into my bag and lay there trying to get some sleep. I was shaking violently and my teeth were chattering but try as I may, I just couldn't get warm. Then I heard some knocking on a door further down the corridor, followed by another knock on a door a bit closer. I expected this to be followed by a shout of, 'Bring out yer dead,' as it certainly couldn't have been room service. Then there was a loud knock on my door. My first thought was that there was a fire in the building, but that would have been wishful thinking on my part! I opened the door slowly and there in front of me was a man with an armful of hot water bottles, his outstretched hand passing me the one thing I craved, heat! I climbed back into the bed with the hot water bottle and as the knocking of doors subsided down the corridor and the hot water bottle heated up my bed, I managed to fall asleep.

I didn't sleep well after the water bottle cooled down and the freezing cold crept back into my bedding. I awoke from my semi-conscious state and thought I was laying next to a dead body until I realised one of my freezing legs was underneath the other. I heard the rain driving hard against the small window in the bathroom and lay there wondering what today would bring. I was feeling exhausted from the last couple of days as all we had seemed to do was ride across rough terrain, eat and sleep. I still managed to feel elated at how well both we and the bikes were holding up.

It was yet another early start for us and after a hearty omelette for breakfast the icy rain stopped and we left the gloomy city of Cerro de Pasco under a cloudy blue sky. The road out of the town was rough and muddy and as I looked back over the depressing sight behind me I realised why the Peruvians there no longer smile. The whole place was thoroughly dispiriting and needed razing to the ground!

When we got to the brow of the mountain, we gradually began to descend and left the greying landscape behind as we wound round the road and into lush tropical vegetation. There had been numerous rockfalls on the road but thankfully they had been cleared enough for us to get past them. The sheer vertical mountainsides were beautiful and were covered in tropical trees. We descended for over an hour and a half through numerous villages.

After a few more miles the road turned to mush and gravel and once again it felt like we had taken a wrong turn onto some farm track. I battled with the handlebars as the Norton slid from side to side underneath me, but *Kate* rose to the challenge and dug in like she had been built for off-roading. The road in front of us had been decimated by numerous rockfalls and landslides and huge earthmovers and excavators were busy moving the rubble, or simply ploughing a new road higher up the mountain from where the original road had slipped down into the valley, due to the heavy rainfall.

We forged numerous fast-flowing streams which cut across the road on their way to the sand coloured river that had now joined our path and was flooding the valley below as it inundated everything in its path. Pete was leading the way and progress was very slow, as the rutted road took its toll on our arms, legs and minds. We were hoping to make it to Pucallpa, from where we would take a boat down the Ucayali River, but with the rough terrain it seemed unlikely we'd get there today.

Then in front of me Pete rode through one of the deep streams that crossed our path and as the water splayed out from his tyre tracks, he juddered to a sharp halt and came off the bike. He had run into a sandbank that the stream had formed and his bike became bogged down and had thrown him! Luckily he was unhurt and the only damage was a broken mirror.

We went on as the road started to climb, heading into numerous tunnels that took us through the mountain and towards Huanuco. Then we went through yet another tunnel that sloped downwards and scared the hell out of me. There was a deep drain to my right and the darkness of the tunnel made it impossible to see as I plodded on behind Pete. Then in front of us appeared bright daylight and what I can only describe as an amazing scene. It was as if we had entered a gateway into the Amazonas and the humidity hit us from the tropical rainforest, which was covered in a mist that kissed the mountain tops. Just looking and smelling the trees, ferns and foliage in front of me was awe inspiring. We stopped the bikes to take in the wonderful scenery and the sight and sounds of insects and animals filled my ears as I breathed in the hot moist air, before eating a sodden stale cheese biscuit I had amazingly found in the bottom my jacket pocket.

The bikes juddered down the unmade road into the valley. We started to pass trucks loaded with logs, the smell of their burning brakes masking the fresh smell of the forest. The sun was shining brightly above us as we began to take stupid risks, overtaking the slow-moving trucks on blind bends to make headway on our journey.

We stopped for a brief lunch at a small village with a population of about 40 people and as we sat outside the only shop (which only sold Inca Cola) we were joined by a congregation of inquisitive children who looked amused by the *gringos* and the ancient bikes we were riding. As we left the village, we passed an armoured police vehicle with its turret pointing towards us, obviously keeping law and order in the sleepy village!

We skipped past Huanuco and on through the village of Chinchao where two rivers met, one green and one sandy red in colour. They joined and rushed ever forward, temporarily accompanying us as we neared Tingo Maria. It was only mid-afternoon but we knew we wouldn't make it to Pucallpa as the roads had slowed our journey considerably, so we stopped at the first hostel we saw in Tingo Maria, the Madera Verde.

Mercedes Monjaras, the administrator of the hostel, showed us to our room, which was a delightful lodge built on stilts and set in beautiful surroundings. Squawking technicoloured parrots seemed to adorn every tree in the fruit-filled garden and the green lawns stretched out to a limestone mountain range behind us, known as the Sleeping Beauty, as it resembles an outstretched naked woman! I felt like we had landed in the Garden of Eden – the place was simply stunning.

Tingo Maria is a relatively small town of approximately 56,000 people and is nicknamed 'The Door to the Amazonia'. It wasn't considered reachable until 1936 when finally a road was built to it. The settlement, with its small wooden houses all built on stilts, focuses on the main square (Plaza de Armas!) which is where Pete and I headed in a small tuk-tuk to have our usual meal of *pollo a la braza et papas* (chicken and chips).

The centre of Tingo Maria was a hive of activity with its maze of shops and stalls selling local produce, from alpaca wool jumpers to every fruit imaginable, as well as sunglasses 'made in Taiwan'. We walked back to our hostel after picking up some wine, beer and cheese biscuits on the way and spent the evening chatting to Mercedes and her colleague Francesca on the front veranda. They were intrigued by our trip, but they warned us that the road from Tingo Maria was infamous for robberies and not to travel at night; also that it wasn't an asphalt road. Judging by the road we had travelled over the last couple of days, I was surprised that they actually knew what an asphalt road was!

After a breakfast of toast and coffee and having added another pint of oil to *Kate's* oil reservoir, we were waved off by Mercedes, Francesca and even Hilda (who made the toast) on the final leg of our journey to Pucallpa. It wasn't long before we hit rain again and the road became very dangerous, as it turned to mud and the bikes struggled for grip. Pete seemed a little grumpy this morning and for the first time on the journey so far, we had a little disagreement when I told him he was beginning to moan about everything. To be fair we were both exhausted, and riding in the torrential downpour was proving very slow and difficult. But it cleared the air between us and relieved the tension that probably builds when two people are together 24/7 in extreme conditions.

Eventually we crossed the Aguatia Bridge which, when Che and Alberto crossed it by truck back in May 1952, was the longest bridge in South America. Asphalt carried on past the bridge for several miles and although we were wet to the skin, it made the ride pleasurable in the humid conditions as we rode through several small villages which weren't even named. Then the trail became very hit and miss as once again the asphalt disappeared, as did the road ahead. Looking through my goggles I could see that the track in front of us had simply slid into the river. Fortunately a giant excavator had dug into the mountainside and constructed a pathway higher up so we could pass through and onward.

There were landslides everywhere and as we approached what I thought was a fork in the road, I looked up to my left and above me I could see two trucks on a road that had replaced the one Pete and I were riding on. The narrow road we were on was cracked and I suddenly realised that most of the road had slipped into the fast flowing river beneath us and that at any moment we could be following suit! We had no option but to carry on, as the road was so narrow we couldn't turn round, so I just gave *Kate* a lot of throttle and prayed we would make it. We were very lucky.

The road was becoming impassable and trucks were parked up in rows, waiting for new roads to be dug. It was only the fact that we were riding motorcycles that allowed us to pass the lengthening convoys. The bikes were being punished and our progress was getting slower and slower as the terrain took its toll on us and we quickly realised we weren't going to make Pucallpa. We eventually stopped at a village called Cuarenta Tres, the village before this one had been named Setenta Dos; they were so small they didn't warrant having a name, they were simply known by how many kilometres they were from Pucallpa!

We found the best hostel in town, in fact we found the only hostel in town and I collapsed exhausted onto the heavily stained mattress, while Pete showered. We then ventured into the village and had our usual evening meal of chicken and chips at a table we shared with three forestry workers, who enjoyed our tales of adventure and the beers we were buying them, into the small hours.

We finally made it to the district of Pucallpa mid-morning, after about an hour's ride thanks to a bit of luck and a long asphalt road! We could tell we were entering suburbia as there was a sudden build-up of tuk-tuk taxis and the road widened to display the driving madness that is the norm in all Peruvian towns and cities.

We then headed towards the river and asked a tuk-tuk driver the way to the port; he waved us towards him and asked us to follow him and showed us the way. As we stopped at one of the roadside entrances to the port we were immediately mobbed by lots of men who didn't seem to have a pair of shoes or a full set of teeth between them. 'Gringo, gringo,' they shouted. The scene was absolutely chaotic, 'Gringo Iquitos, gringo Iquitos.' They knew where we were going because this was the end of the road and the only way out of Pucallpa was back the way we had come, or by boat, down the Ucuyali River to Iquitos.

A small fight broke out among a couple of the men as they vied for our trade and the rest of the shouting hoard led us to some big steel gates which were flung open to reveal a very muddy dockside and numerous riverboats moored on the muddy banks of the Ucuyali River. There were lots of trucks being unloaded by hand and their loads of toilet roll and nappies were being carried aboard a boat called *Tuky*, which according to the board hanging off the bridge, sailed 'Hoy 5 p.m.' We were in luck. Not only was it was sailing that day but we had time to organise food and drink for our trip. But first things first, we had to negotiate a price for us and the bikes and this was where Pete's diplomatic expertise would come in.

Pete had read in his guide book that the only person you negotiated with was the captain of the vessel. I stood

Asados, an Argentine family tradition, with my Argentine 'family' in Choele Choel.

Our typical sleeping arrangements, in San Martin de los Andes, Argentina.

Gustavo Agra and a movie star Norton see us off on our adventure! (Argentina)

On the vast plains of the Argentine Pampas.

Crossing the Tropic of Capricorn in Chile.

We eventually stole the limelight from the Nortons in Santiago, Chile, where we were interviewed for the local news.

The route of the seven lakes in Argentina – simply stunning.

The sights and culture in Argentina were intoxicating.

Sleeping with 'Kate' in the Atacama, Chile.

A size 6 cactus thorn in my size 8 boot ... ouch! (Chile)

Two old-timers ... and two old bikes, in Chile.

A free-for-all as the market starts onboard the deck of the *Tuky* in Peru.

Machu Picchu, the lost Incan city, which we found quite easily.

No mas estrellas (no more stars), a Colombian shrine to a traffic accident victim.

There was even sand in my underwear (not shown!).

It didn't take me long to discover that riding at night in Peru could and would be very dangerous.

The Nortons are dug out and rescued after the sandstorm in Ica, Peru.

watch over the bikes while Pete walked across the thick muddy bank and asked for the captain.

A small fat bloke wearing an imitation Chelsea shirt and with what looked like a tight perm, appeared on the deck and looked down at Pete on the bank. 'How much for two people and two motorcycles, to Iquitos?' Pete shouted up at him. He looked preoccupied with the lads who were loading the nappies into the hold and barked some orders at them in Spanish, totally ignoring Pete's question. Pete walked up the plank onto the deck of *Tuky* and stood next to the captain, who was much smaller than him. The captain took no notice of him as he shouted more orders to his deckhands, he then arrogantly beckoned Pete over to a table and two chairs which were on the deck and they sat down to haggle over a price.

The bikes were put in the hold and we were shown to our cabin, which was basically a cooler house with two bunks. Pete had successfully got us a cabin at the same price we would have paid to sleep in a hammock on board and was rather pleased with the outcome of his and the fat captain's bartering. We had enough time to go into the centre of Pucallpa and stock up on essentials from the local supermarket for our three-day boat trip to Iquitos. We bought enough beer, wine, bread and tuna fish to last us three days, then walked back to the *Tuky* and sat on board drinking beer while we waited to sail. It was obviously going to be a night sailing and I eventually fell asleep to the gentle rocking of the riverboat.

Chapter 16
The *Tuky*

The stench of sweat filled the cabin. I jumped off the top bunk and opened the door to let in some fresh air and my jaw dropped. We were still moored at the riverbank in Pucallpa. The movements I had felt in the night were probably more boats arriving and bumping their way into the line of riverboats already moored. The riverbank had turned into a muddy bog as the torrential rain had fallen relentlessly through the night and yet the young crew members kept on unloading the slow stream of wagons that somehow managed to reverse down the slippery bank.

'When do we sail?' I hollered at a young lad who was carrying the equivalent of his body weight in Inca Cola onto the *Tuky*. 'Hoy, five o'clock,' came the smiling response. I began to wonder if this was a three-day boat journey to Iquitos or if it was a boat journey to Iquitos that sailed in three days.

I looked down at the murky, silty waters of the Ucuyali in which Che and Alberto had swum before their departure aboard their riverboat, *La Cenepa*. It was strewn with floating trees that had slipped into the river with the many landslides. The trees and debris were making far better progress down the river than we were and we resigned ourselves to spending another day in Pucallpa.

Then, what I can only describe as a 'lady boy', a very effeminate looking man appeared on the deck outside our cabin. The perfect complexion, unblemished make-up and manicured eyebrows were framed by neatly styled shoulder-length blonde hair. The purple paisley mini-dress was complemented by a pair of tight-fitting purple jeans, which saved his blushes and mine!

'Desayuno?' he pouted towards Pete, his red lips pursing in a kissing motion.

Pete looked at him horrified and bewildered, not understanding what he meant or wanted and we both looked at each other and somehow managed to stifle our giggles.

'Desayuno?' he repeated, motioning with his hands as if he was reeling in a fish from the river below us. The penny finally dropped. This was the boat's cook and he wanted to know if we wanted breakfast. 'Si, si,' we replied in harmony and proceeded to follow the cook towards the galley in the bowels of the *Tuky*.

We sat down at a table with the crew members of the boat and waited to see what culinary delights our camp cook had conjured up. He soon produced a large bowl of rice soup, out of which protruded what looked like a deformed chicken leg without the meat. He ladled the soup into the passenger's bowls first (me and Pete) and then let the young crew members help themselves. I didn't touch mine as it didn't look very appetising and instead offered it to the crew member next to me, whose eyes lit up like he had won the lottery as he gulped it down heartily.

I looked at all the plastic bottles, rubbish and waste that was floating on the river around the boat and decided not to take a shower. The water in the toilet, shower and sink was a horrible brown colour as the supply came straight out of the river. It wouldn't have made me any cleaner, and I didn't want to catch Legionnaire's disease. Why Che and Alberto had swum in the Ucuyali was beyond me!

As our boat wasn't sailing until five in the afternoon we decided to take a look around Pucallpa and perhaps get something decent to eat. We hailed one of the tuk-tuks which were parked outside the large dock gates and headed into the town.

Pucallpa is a small city which is located in the north-east of Peru, not far from the Brazilian border and is isolated by the Andes mountain range and the Amazon rainforest. The road on which we had ridden into Pucallpa was completed in 1945 and allowed commercialisation of the port city and access to the rest of the country. The heavy rain, flash floods and landslides we had ridden through regularly destroy the road and often cut it off from the rest of Peru for short periods.

We walked aimlessly round Pucallpa, its intricate maze of streets lined with vendors selling colourful fruits from their makeshift stalls, to the backdrop of the many clothes shops selling counterfeit T-shirts and sports bags. The horns of thousands of tuk-tuk taxis filled the contaminated air as they whizzed round the concrete roads looking for trade, and it was mesmerising to watch the traffic lights at the main junctions change to green and start what looked like a tuk-tuk race, as hundreds of them set off leaving a plume of thick black smoke in their wake. We spent the whole of the day just skulking round the labyrinth of shops before stocking up on more red wine and beer at the local supermarket and heading back to the *Tuky*.

Our captain was outside the shanty bar (which for some strange reason was named the Los Angeles Bar) on the riverbank across from the *Tuky*, so I decided to go join him for a beer and ask him when we would be sailing. I entered the makeshift bar and stared at the uneven baked mud floor, then at the old wooden stools and tables, and then I helped myself to a beer from the tall refrigerator that stood in the corner. The walls of the bar were made from plywood and corrugated sheets and the roof was just a tarpaulin sheet from a truck; the only thing of value was the refrigerator and the bottles of beer that were rammed tightly into it.

'Would you like a beer captain?' I motioned to the fridge.

'No,' came his abrupt reply, which was colder than the beer I had in my hand.

I walked over to the fridge, grabbed another beer and handed it to him.

'I don't like to drink alone and it's rude to enter a bar and not buy a drink,' I told him.

He cracked a smile and took the beer; I think the ice had finally melted.

'You are from Germany?'

'No, England. The north of England.' I quickly changed the subject, 'Are we going to be sailing soon?'

'Who knows, maybe tomorrow? The road from Lima has suffered rockfalls, floods and mudslides and is holding up all the trucks. We are in the lap of the gods.'

Then torrential rain began to beat hard on the tarpaulin roof which held firm and did its job.

'If this continues it will be difficult to keep the road open,' and with that, he swigged the last of his beer, mumbled something about the rain in England and then disappeared into the rainy night.

I spent the rest of the evening on deck with Pete, drinking red wine and eating the supplies we had bought for the three-day boat journey. The clock tower on the plaza was lit up and music blared out loudly from a cluster of speakers that towered above the shanty dockside as we relaxed and talked about our journey, the joys and dangers of our trip and slowly, we got drunk.

There was a knock on the door of our cabin, 'Desayuno,

desayuno.' It was our friend the cook letting us know that breakfast was about to be served in the galley. We were joined at the breakfast table by a young American family, who were travelling down into the Amazon region to preach Christianity to the locals. The lettering on the father's navy T-shirt explained all, reading: 'Messenger of God'. Then the cook served us his speciality, rice soup and a rice drink. I thought it was absolutely amazing what that boy could do with rice. The messenger of God then said grace and thanked the Lord for what we were about to receive, and we rather ungratefully threw the tasteless rice soup overboard where it belonged, to feed the fish!

I was slowly going stir crazy sat aboard the *Tuky* just waiting to sail. The day dragged and I missed riding *Kate* on the open roads. After *La Poderosa* was left behind, Che and Alberto's journey and destinations had been dictated to them by the lifts they had hitched aboard trucks after their motorcycle had broken down, whereas until now we'd had the choice and freedom of choosing where we wanted to ride. Now, aboard the *Tuky*, we were under the same constraints as Che and Alberto and I felt frustrated by the delays which were totally beyond our control. The highlight of my day was a shower in the brown polluted waters of the Ucuyali and a change of clothes. An early night beckoned as I climbed into my bunk and prayed to God we would be sailing soon. The American family's message had got through to me!

'Mission from God' read today's T-shirt as the American bid us good morning, and it was a beautiful morning. It was the 28th February, and even though we were still moored at the riverbank, the sign on the *Tuky* had been changed to '*Tuky*. Hoy 3.30. Sin Falte'. Even with my limited Spanish I knew that they hadn't organised an Irish night on board! The *Tuky* would be sailing at 3.30 today, without fail.

As if by some miracle, trucks and pick-ups arrived in their droves and their payload was unloaded quickly and carried onto the deck of our boat, from where it was loaded into the hold. Lots of slabs of ice were packed into boxes of sawdust to insulate the hold from the heat and keep the cargo cool. Then lots of passengers started to board and the *Tuky* looked like it had giant ants pouring onto its decks, as they fought for the little space left on the upper deck on which to hang their hammocks. People were milling everywhere and vendors boarded to sell their wares to the passengers. Fresh fruit, biscuits, water, home made pastries and hammocks were all snapped up by the commuters heading home or simply travelling down river. Below us steel, different types of engines, ice, nappies, cement mixers and more ice were being loaded. The boat was crammed and still cargo was being brought on board, as children and dogs scampered all over the decks bewildered at the chaos surrounding them.

Then as the pointed clock in the plaza read 4.55, the gangplanks were pulled on board and we slowly reversed away from the muddy bank and started to make our way up the Ucuyali, followed by a small flotilla of *peque-peques* still trying to sell their wares to the passengers. Within half a mile the *Tuky* docked against the muddy riverbank once more, as we took on more passengers and a huge crane that was waiting in the shadows loaded some heavy steel sheets on to the already overloaded deck. It was 6.15 by the plaza clock when we finally set sail and this time navigation was by the searchlight which shone out brightly from the bridge into the darkness of the night and attracted thousands of flies and mosquitoes. We were finally on our way. *Sin falte!*

Our small two berth cabin was sandwiched in-between two larger four berth cabins one of which was occupied by the American evangelists and the other by a Peruvian mother and her young children, Hernandez and his slightly older sister Isabella, who were very noisy and very demanding of their guardian. She obviously doted on her offspring and saw to their every need, and food seemed to be Hernandez's main need! The children seemed confused by the *gringos* as Pete and I sat on two plastic chairs just staring out at the darkness that was the Amazon rainforest and relaxing with a cup of red wine each.

I thought about when Alberto and Che had set sail on this very river all those years ago towards the Loreto region, then Iquitos and how they would have seen the exact same sights down the Ucuyali as we would be seeing. I was excited at the prospect of seeing the mighty Amazon and its one and a half billion acres of rainforest, but most of all I was just glad we were on our way. We had been on the *Tuky* for three days without moving and now we had another three days on the boat before we got to Iquitos.

The sound of what I thought was a tambourine got louder and louder and I woke up in a hot sweat. The humidity of the rainforest and the closeness of our cabin walls made the conditions on board very uncomfortable. I jumped off my bunk and flung the cabin door open to let some air in, but with a relative humidity of about 85 per cent it didn't make the slightest difference and the perspiration rolled down my face and back. A mist rose off the Ucuyali River and made for poor visibility but I could just about make out the rainforest on both sides of the riverbank where there was lots of floating debris including trees, bamboo and lots of plastic bottles. Every now and then I would catch the odd glimpse of a tall thatched house built high on stilts to combat the rise and fall of the river in the rainy season.

Then the tambourines started up again but this time they were real. Below me on the open deck lots of Peruvian women in identical traditional dress, started to sing hymns in melodic harmony to the slow beat of the hand-held pandereta. It was Sunday, 1st March, and even though these staunch Catholics were stuck on our delayed boat they still managed to worship at the church of *Tuky*. It was a very moving sight, to see that they had all met on the deck for Sunday worship and had dressed up for the occasion.

That was until the American evangelist appeared, prised one of the tambourines off a startled looking young girl and proceeded to speed up the tempo of the hymn into a frenzy. His enthusiasm and lack of South American ways was all too apparent as the young choir did their best to keep up with the rhythm he was now vigorously banging on the tambourine as if he was in a trance. The messenger of God eventually went solo as the young girls struggled to keep up with the pace of the pulsating beat and watched in awe and amazement as the American shared the word of God like a demented punk rocker. 'Hallelujah, Hallelujah,' he chanted, then he finished with a burst of 'Praise the Lord and Thanks be to God,' to a rapturous standing round of applause from his appreciative audience. It was amazing to watch as the evangelist had them eating out of his hand and I had no doubt his unorthodox approach would be a great success in Peru, along with his catchphrase T-shirts.

We eventually docked at a place called Contamana where a brass band played on the riverside to welcome the boat, as hundreds of passengers disembarked and hundreds more embarked carrying mattresses and hammocks and all their worldly possessions. More cargo was placed on board and I was sure the *Tuky* must be down to its Plimsoll line and severely overloaded, as the decks were now packed to the rafters.

On we sailed down the weaving river which threaded north through the lush forest, leaving behind hundreds of ox-bow lakes where the river had eroded the muddy banks over hundreds of years. We seemed to stop every five minutes at each small farm for squealing pigs and bamboo crates full of clucking chickens to somehow be stacked on the deck in what little space was left. Then further up river, cows and bulls were brought aboard. It was amusing to watch the deckhands trying to cajole the two ton beasts to make the five foot leap onto the deck from the riverbank without the use of a ramp. Then it became sickening to watch as a lot of the cattle panicked and lay down. Force was then used in the form of tail twisting, kicking and plastic bags being tied round their nostrils so they couldn't breathe, and they became so distressed they jumped aboard the *Tuky*, where they were dragged by rope and kicked into the hold where our bikes were!

The mosquitoes seemed angrier than usual that evening, as the low crimson sunlight bounced off the Ucuyali and gave the river a blood red colour. Above us, the sky was powder pink and pastel blue among the fading white clouds as the biting gnats set to work on my bare arms and legs. The captain appeared with a can of spray and proceeded to spray into all three cabins on our deck. Whether it was insect killer to see off the mosquitoes or air freshener to nullify the smell of sweat, it didn't work.

I hardly slept a wink that night; a mix of the humidity, the grunting of the pigs on deck, the mosquitoes and the frequent stops kept me wide awake. I went down to the makeshift serving hatch among all the hammocks and ordered a beer then sat and enjoyed the evening with two very drunk Peruvians who found this white Englishman a great source of amusement.

The next two days aboard the *Tuky* just blurred into each other. It was rice for breakfast, dinner and supper, all of which went into the river to feed the fish, and then a carton of red wine before bed. We had been on board for seven nights and I felt like a prisoner. Hernandez, the boy in the cabin next to ours seemed content. He smiled a lot, probably due to the never-ending supply of food from his mother.

The scenery along the Ucuyali changed very little. It was rainforest all the way, with only the cry of parrots, the intermittent sound of chattering monkeys and the odd small village. We made hundreds of stops as every individual on board seemed to have a different destination. The only scenery that did change was on the deck of the boat, as steel and cement mixers were replaced by fish, crocodile meat and goat's legs, which were packed in ice, then thousands of bright yellow bananas on which the starving pigs did their best to feed.

At 4 a.m. on the 4th March, we stopped again, this time it was because of thick fog in which the pilot of the boat had run us aground. We were firmly stuck on a sandbank and he was out on the deck protesting his innocence to the snarling captain below. I noticed a rifle next to the wheel on the bridge of the boat. There was no radio, no maps, but a rifle? I tried to work out what it was for. A great ape attack? Perhaps it was in case there was a mutiny among the crew or even to ward off over-zealous vendors mounting the boat in great numbers, to sell their produce? No. Apparently it was in case anybody fell overboard – the rifle would be used to shoot any approaching crocodiles. All I can say is if the pilot's shooting was anything like his steering I would sooner take my chances with the crocs!

Eventually with the use of poles and a lot of high revving of the overworked diesel engine, the crew managed to free us from the sandbank. As we rounded the next bend in the river, we could make out the lights of quite a large city in the distance. We had finally reached Iquitos.

Chapter 17
The mighty Amazon

As the early morning sun rose above the thick river mist it lit up the distant city of Iquitos, a place which is only accessible by boat or small airplane. It was 5 a.m. and on board the *Tuky* the decks were crammed with passengers shouting and whistling as we approached the harbour. It was our final stopping point where all remaining passengers were due to disembark. A small flotilla of *peque-peques* had already gathered next to us ready to sell their wares and as I looked at the port ahead, I was overwhelmed. The muddy banks were lined with hundreds of people dressed in bright colours, shouting, waving and waiting to greet us. Then I looked at the tightly packed riverboats which were harboured against the riverbank, they left absolutely no room for us to dock and I wondered where we would be able to moor the huge vessel that had been our home for the past seven days.

This is where the expertise of our pilot and all those years of hitting the riverbank came into practice. We approached the huge stern of another riverboat at a 45 degree angle and gently rammed it to make a small gap into which our daring navigator then prised an opening with the *Tuky's* bow. The sound of scraping metal was drowned out by the loud blast of the *Tuky's* claxon as it shrieked out in victorious triumph at finding a place to moor. The other boats rocked violently sideways as the *Tuky* forced her way into the ever widening gap that she had bludgeoned open for herself and very slowly we approached the muddy dockside.

With little regard for their personal safety the waiting dockside crowd started to pour on board the *Tuky* before she had docked and it was mayhem as hundreds of people clambered onto the deck. The boxes containing the fish were burst open and eager women tightly clutching straw baskets filled them with fish which were then weighed and sold on board! We had an on board market, a free for all and utter chaos. Bamboo cages full of chickens were smashed open and they were sold to the waiting punters, while the few squealing pigs left on board were dragged off by their hind legs to their fate.

My reunion with *Kate* would have to wait as there was no chance of unloading any cargo off the *Tuky*. The crowds were fighting to get on board to buy fish, crocodile, chickens and whatever else was hidden in the ice-packed boxes on board. We were told we would be able to get the bikes when the crowd had dispersed, so we left the madness of the *Tuky* and got a mototaxi to the next dock to try to find a boat to take us and our bikes to Leticia, Colombia.

At the next dockside we were mobbed by the usual hangers on and fixers trying to make a fast sol, but once again negotiated with the fat captain of a huge blue boat bound for Santa Rosa which is the last place in Peru on the Amazon. He told us to be back at the boat with the bikes after 3 p.m. and that his boat was sailing first thing in the morning.

For the first time in over a week we had a breakfast that didn't consist of rice! Fresh orange juice, toast and freshly ground *café con leche* was served to us as we sat at a café on the beautiful Plaza de Armas in the centre of Iquitos. It is dominated by the beautiful clock tower of the Iglesia Matriz, a daunting Gothic church situated on the delightful square which is lined with beautiful colonial buildings built during the rubber boom years of the early twentieth century. The crowded restaurants and shops gave the square an almost European feel, if you ignore the humid heat and the constant noise of the tuk-tuks blasting their ear-bursting horns.

Back at the *Tuky* the thriving on board market had subsided and the decks were almost bare, save for a few empty fish boxes. Pete and I got our things together and went to the lower deck where our bikes were still parked in the cattle hold, along with several cows and bulls. I inspected *Kate* as I hadn't seen her in a while and now noticed she had no back light lens, which must have got knocked off when the deckhands were herding the cattle on board. My Norton now had no lights at all!

The captain was squeezed behind a small desk adjacent to where we were stood and beckoned us over to where he sat. 'You have to pay for the motorcycles,' he mumbled while scribbling on a notepad he had in front of him. There was a long silence and I could see Pete's face slowly turn to anger. 'We shook hands, we had a deal, we specifically agreed a price before we sailed,' Pete shouted at him. 'The price was for two persons only, it did not include the motorcycles,' he retorted. Pete was furious and I looked on open mouthed as he told the captain in no uncertain terms, 'You are a lying, robbing, scheming, fat, greasy-haired slime-ball, we sorted a price out before we sailed and you know it!'

The captain looked shocked at Pete's outburst and whatever payment he had in mind had probably trebled. 'No, no, you pay for...' but before he could finish the sentence Pete walked away from him in disgust. The captain looked at him, then shrugged his shoulders, but Pete wasn't having any of it.

We certainly had no bargaining powers as our bikes were still on board the boat and there was no way we would be able off-load them onto the bank without the assistance of the deckhands. I looked at Pete and put my hand reassuringly on his shoulder, 'Let's just pay him and get the hell out of here, we need to get to the next boat,' I told him. 'How much? Two motorcycles?' Pete turned from me and snapped at the captain.

We parted company with 100 sols each and were stood on the muddy riverbank loading our luggage onto the bikes when the heavens opened and turned the dockside into a quagmire. It rained so hard we were soaked to the skin in seconds and as I looked towards the *Tuky* and to the deck where the captain's desk was sheltered I could see him looking down at us with a huge smirk spread across his face.

It felt good to be riding *Kate* again, albeit in the rain and only for a few hundred yards to the next dock. I hadn't realised how much I had missed her and I felt a great sense of freedom after being cooped up aboard the *Tuky* for the last few days. The Norton's tyres cut through the thick muddy riverbank with an expertise I had almost forgotten, as she slipped and nearly spilled me off before she finally gripped and we were on our way to the next dock to find the boat which would take us down river and even deeper into the Amazon rainforest.

As we rode onto the dock I started to look for the big blue boat we were due to sail in for the remainder of the journey down the river, but there was a huge gap where the vessel bound for Santa Rosa had been docked and Pete and I looked at each other, horrified at our predicament. Had it sailed without us? Were we at the right dock even?

Then I heard a familiar voice shouting, 'Steve, Steve.' I looked over to where several other boats were moored and could just barely make out a waving figure among the hundreds of people milling on the dockside. It was Juana, the mother of Hernandez and Isabella, who had been in the cabin next to us on board the *Tuky*. I parked the bike and ran over to where she stood. 'Steve, this boat sails tonight at seven o'clock bound for Santa Rosa, you must get on board it. Come I will take you to the captain.' She then handed a huge sandwich to Hernandez and I followed the three of them up the gangplank of the brightly painted *Carlos Antonio*.

The first thing I noticed on board the *Carlos Antonio* was the captain. He was fat, sweating and looked like all the other riverboat captains we had come across. It was like a bad dream and I wondered if all the captains on the boats sailing up and down the Amazon were somehow related to each other. Then I looked at Hernandez; he had devoured the *bocadillo* his mother had given him and was now working his way through a huge ear of corn. The future could only hold one career prospect for young 'captain' Hernandez.

Juana then negotiated with the captain of the *Carlos Antonio* on my behalf. There was a lot of hand waving and raised voices most of which I didn't understand apart from the captain's use of the word *gringo* several times, which I knew meant a much higher price. But Juana was having none of it and let him know as much by calling him a 'pirate'. Then Juana turned round smiling and gave me an acknowledging nod. She had struck a deal with the captain to take us and the bikes to Santa Rosa at very favourable Peruvian rates. Juana could certainly multi-task!

Pete and I, and our newly adopted family settled on the top deck of the *Carlos Antonio* where we tied our hammocks to the rafters of the vast open deck. There were no cabins aboard the *Carlos Antonio* so we were in 'steerage class' and besides it seemed almost romantic to be sailing down the Amazon while gently dozing on a swinging hammock.

The hammocks we had recently purchased from a local vendor were made from nylon cord, but everyone else aboard the boat seemed to have the luxury drape model.

Juana unfolded hers from a carpet bag she was carrying and using the knot-tying skills of an old seadog soon had her three opulent cradles swinging from the stanchions that formed the structure of the canopy of the boat. Within minutes young Hernandez had miraculously managed to leap from the deck and nestle into his hammock while munching on a chocolate bar as he pulled the tasselled sides in and swung from side to side like a contented cocooned butterfly.

The bright yellow and blue nylon cord hammock I had purchased seemed to lose all its appeal as I leapt onto it in a similar movement (minus the chocolate bar) and somehow performed a very delicate balancing act to prevent myself from twisting right over and onto the deck below. I managed to reassure myself that as long as I didn't breathe the hammock would somehow stay upright.

Foot passengers were now boarding the *Carlos Antonio* in their hundreds and quickly staked their claim for the limited sleeping space. They tied their hammocks at every angle and in every space available. There were hammocks above me, hammocks below me and they were so tightly packed together I had no chance of falling out or even getting out without asking at least a dozen people to let me pass! The one consolation was that we were at the front of the passenger compartment and next to the one television that served the whole deck.

With the bikes loaded on the front deck of the *Carlos Antonio* and covered in a plastic sheet, we decided to go into Iquitos and grab something decent to eat before our seven o'clock sailing. We found an American restaurant named The Yellow Rose of Texas which boasted 'the best steaks in Peru' and as I had been eating from the 'hundred things to do with rice' menu for the last seven days I had what tasted like the best steak in the whole world!

We had a look round the brightly coloured streets of the Amazonian city and walking back through Plaza de Armas to get a taxi we came across a building known as La Casa de Fierro (The Iron House). It was designed by Gustave Eiffel, of Eiffel Tower fame. It was beautifully preserved and housed a café and the Iquitos social club. It is thought to be the first prefabricated house in the Americas and was, amazingly, carried through the jungle by hundreds of men, then sailed down the Amazon before being assembled in Iquitos in 1890 for some wealthy rubber baron.

It was time to get back to the boat. The sun was slowly disappearing along the blushing waters of the Amazon and we boarded the *Carlos Antonio* and stood next to the Nortons, which were silhouetted against the ruby sky. We watched as the pilot skilfully navigated the enormous riverboat between the other moored boats and out of the busy harbour and on schedule we slipped out of Iquitos and headed down the Amazon towards our final destination in Peru.

The river got wider and wider and the banks of the Amazon disappeared into the distance as darkness fell and we went up on deck to our hammocks and settled in them for the night. I cuddled my rucksack to prevent it going missing and also as a source of safety, as the ancient TV which was directly above my hammock didn't look very safe on the rusty bracket that was holding it to the wall. It was switched on and silence fell around me as a Chuck Norris film started on the grainy screen above.

Then suddenly the loudest thunder I had ever heard, quickly followed by a huge flashbulb of lightning lighting up the whole sky, warned us of the storm we were sailing towards. I lay on my hammock and remembered my father comforting me when I was a child, telling me that 'the thunder in the sky was God riding his chariot across heaven to find his disciples'. Well, on this occasion he must have attached extra horses and rode six in hand pulling a fully loaded Wells Fargo stagecoach across the sky, as the noise was absolutely deafening. The lights went out on the boat for a few brief seconds and Chuck Norris disappeared from the TV. Then driving rain lashed onto the deck and those in the hammocks nearest to the sides leapt out of them and quickly dropped the tarpaulin sheets which were in place to protect us from the elements.

A young girl who was directly in front of me had her arms round two small hens who were sharing her hammock and she looked at me cuddling my rucksack before letting out a huge smile. I smiled back realising how ridiculous I must look, trussed up on little more than a clothes line for a bed, seeking comfort from a huge backpack while watching a Chuck Norris DVD dubbed into Spanish.

I didn't sleep a wink that first night aboard the *Carlos Antonio*. The cold wind cut through the open deck and a 6,000 watt light bulb, which had surely been meant for a lighthouse on the coast, was shining brightly above me and attracted more flying objects than London Heathrow. The whole back catalogue of Chuck's movies was played and I harked back to our first few days on South American soil when I had thought that Dakar Motos in Buenos Aires left a lot to be desired. Compared to what we had endured over the last couple of weeks it was pure luxury and I found myself wishing I was back on the top bunk in the suburban garage instead of in the hammock that was cutting deep into my skin.

All night there was a constant stream of people going to and fro as stops were made at the numerous remote hamlets that were built on the riverbank. I had to get out of the hammock every hour or so anyway just to get the circulation back into my legs and on doing so woke everybody in my immediate vicinity as I nudged one hammock and it started a chain reaction, nudging the one next to it and so forth.

Morning came with the squawking of macaws flying overhead as the warm sun finally peeked over the distant horizon and lit up the rainforest basin. It was a case of one up, all up, as the hammocks once again rocked in unison and the occupants rose from the comfort of their bedding looking refreshed after a good night's sleep.

The *Carlos Antonio* seemed to be making stops every hundred yards or so, as the rainforest was so thick and the bank was only accessible by boat, making walking from village to village nigh on impossible. We had a brief 15 minute stop at the place where Che and Alberto visited the leprosarium of San Pablo, but we couldn't get off to take a look as the boat wouldn't have been docked there when we got back and besides, there was no road on which to ride the bikes. As doctors, Che and Alberto spent 12 days working at the San Pablo leper colony before carrying on their journey down river on a raft they named the Mambo-Tango. It was either a very brave or very stupid thing to do; the river is vast and the currents very dangerous.

The rest of the day just paled into rainforest and river with the monotony broken by a boarding from a Peruvian customs officer who wanted to check our papers. As we sailed down the Amazon I stared out at the villages we passed and what did stand out for me was the way the locals depend on the river. They fish in it, sail their wares up and down on it and even wash in it; one elderly local woman, seemingly oblivious to the huge, brightly coloured boat docked next to her, stripped and dunked her large breasts into the river one by one before washing her whole body in the brown murky waters.

The bland rice we were served for breakfast, dinner and supper gave us a brief reminder and a flashback to our time on the *Tuky*. The cook on the *Carlos Antonio* must have taken a shine to Pete, as his rice drink in the evening had a little addition which at first looked like a huge chunk of meat. It was in fact a huge stewed cockroach which he threw into the river along with the drink.

Stops were becoming even more regular as every passenger on board seemed to have a different destination and it was easy to work out why the Amazon River was so wide. The guy who was piloting the boat seemed to have the knack of running the *Carlos Antonio* into the riverbank at great speed to stop the boat, which on many occasions grounded us for a short while. This allowed those passengers who wanted to get off ample time to do so, but very likely suffering from a whiplash injury as everybody was thrown violently forward as we gouged yet another chunk out of the riverbank. Whatever happened to the idea of reversing the boat's engine to slow it down?

We were due to dock at Santa Rosa early the following morning and our last night on board the *Carlos Antonio* was no different from the night before as the cold night air bit deep into my bones aided by the nylon netted hammock I had chosen for my bed. The back-to-back Kung-Fu films showing on the battered old TV above me once again had what was left of the passengers transfixed. I finally managed to doze off during the night's third showing of *Under Siege*.

I awoke at about five in the morning as there was a lot of shouting going on below us on the main deck. The pilot had somehow managed to get us stuck on a mudbank close to the side of the river. The crew were pushing poles deep into the riverbed to try to free the boat and the engine was revving so high I thought it would blow at any minute. The gearbox banged and clunked from reverse to drive then reverse again in a feeble attempt to free us. The young crew were running round the decks shouting at each other in utter disarray and seemed unsure as to what to do. Then the fat captain appeared on the bridge bleary eyed and infuriated as he attempted to restore order. He barked out some orders and dragged the pilot by his shirt from behind the steering wheel as he shouted and cursed and then proceeded to repeat what the pilot had been doing. The boat shuddered once more from the effects of the gearbox being rammed from forward to aft as a cloud of thick black smoke plumed from the boat's turquoise funnel and momentarily blotted out the rising sun. Perhaps this was a regular occurrence and was the real reason Che and Alberto had continued their journey by raft. Their decision didn't seem as foolish as I had first thought. Then the boat's engine was shut down and I realised that we were well and truly stuck.

We were marooned for over two hours, but no one on board seemed overly concerned. The passengers carried on as normal swinging away in their hammocks and feeding the wildlife on board. Juana maternally saw to the needs of her young, producing yet another item of food from the seemingly bottomless carpet bags she had with her! The cook did his rounds and served everyone with the usual meal of rice as Pete and I looked at each other before throwing it in tandem overboard to feed the fish once more. Santa Rosa seemed an eternity away at that moment.

Then the captain appeared with an armful of charts and spread them on a table next to the steering wheel on the bridge. I was impressed; it seemed there was more to being a riverboat captain than eating lots of food and getting fat. He was joined by a couple of younger crew members who hung on his every word and within minutes they dispersed from the meeting and began to run round the lower deck shouting at their mates. The long poles on board were pushed into the mudbank off the port side of the boat with two crew members to a pole. They looked like giant oars on a Viking ship that would be able to row us out of our predicament. Then the captain once more sparked the *Carlos Antonio's* diesel propulsion engine into life as the propeller at the back of the boat spun wildly and skipped a series of huge ripples across the surface of the river. The boat's gearbox clicked and clunked once more and the crew members drove their poles into the mudbank which, after a few minutes, very slowly released us from her grasp. Besides me and Pete, the captain was the only person on board who looked relieved at us escaping from the riverbed as he passed the wheel over to the pilot and grudgingly left the bridge. His charts of the river had been very accurate.

We were some six hours behind our scheduled docking time but as the passengers left the boat on our many stops, numbers on board gradually declined and it was possible to walk round the deck that had previously been packed to the rafters with hammocks and hens. We got off at a place called Santa Maria where we sat at a café on the riverside and had a coffee and bought some cheese biscuits while we watched some of the boat's cargo being unloaded. Our bikes were now alone on the deck, save for some oil drums.

Back on board we set sail and passed through lots of channels where river dolphins congregated in their dozens but were too shy to come near the boat. On we sailed and it was around 1.15 p.m. when the small port of Santa Rosa appeared in the far distance and everybody on board wrapped up their hammocks, got their belongings together and made ready to disembark. We finally docked in Santa Rosa at about 2.30 p.m. and were boarded by the usual teams of hangers-on and officials. We were told to wait on board until the customs officer cleared us to take the bikes off the boat and we took the opportunity to say goodbye to Juana and her young family who were carrying on down river on another boat to Brazil.

Then a young lad boarded the boat with a couple of friends and introduced himself to us as George. He spoke very good English and told us he had a boat and could get us through customs and into Leticia with the bikes for 40 sols. It sounded too good to be true!

Chapter 18
Illegal entry

We walked down the gangplank onto the riverbank and we were in Santa Rosa de Yavari (to give it its full title). It consisted of a small wooden police station with a thatched roof, a slightly bigger customs office constructed of wood with a tin sheet roof and a couple of other outbuildings, which must have served passengers on their way down river into Brazil. These were the only other buildings visible in this last small outpost and checkpoint of Peru which isn't even shown on the map.

After getting our usual stamps and paperwork from the police office, passport control and the customs office, we were officially cleared to leave Peru. Looking across the Amazon to our left was the town of Leticia. It is Colombia's southern-most town and was where we were heading for. To the right of Leticia is the small town of Tabatinga in Brazil and the area where these three countries come together is known locally as Tres Fronteras. All three countries have fought wars over many years for the small isolated towns they each now possess on the banks of the Amazon which are only accessible by river.

Our main problem was getting the bikes off the boat and onto the riverside. The deck of the *Carlos Antonio* was about seven feet above us and the gangplank looked way too narrow and steep for the bikes to come down. George, the young lad who was to take us across to Colombia had moored his motorised canoe next to the vast riverboat and herded a few willing youths together. Between them they managed to lift and slide Pete's Norton down the gangplank without any damage and onto terra firma. *Kate* proved a little more difficult for them, as my pannier bags were a little wider, and showing little disregard for her she was forced down the gangplank despite my appeals to be gentle and all the buckles and straps were ripped off my leather bags.

The next challenge was to get the two bikes (with a combined weight of about half a ton) onto George's small motorised canoe as there was no other way to cross to Colombia. Pete's Norton was lifted on first and put at the front of the canoe with very little effort. Then with a lot of lifting, pushing and pulling mine was somehow dropped on board and slotted tightly behind Pete's bike on the small craft. Unfortunately the canoe was now very low in the water and I wondered if we would be able to make it across the Amazon to Leticia.

We paid the helpers a few sols each and managed to squeeze in-between the bikes and board the canoe. Once George and his friend had got in we set off for Colombia. We were in a canoe that had been designed for five people and I had visions of us sinking, along with the bikes, as the water was dangerously high and lapping worryingly into the boat. George let up on the gas and gently nursed the boat to the nearest point of Leticia, where he managed to dock us at a rotting wooden jetty, where there were old wooden shanty houses and other small canoes which were being loaded with bananas.

Lots of people gathered at the jetty as we landed to see what was happening and helped us to lift the bikes off the canoe for a small fee. Then a small fight broke out and mayhem followed as the locals fought over the money we had paid them for helping us. Before we knew it four policemen armed with machine guns arrived on two motorcycles and one of them menacingly waved his gun in our faces and demanded to see our papers. 'Where is your stamp?' he asked us, while the other three, waving their guns from side to side went to see what all the commotion was about on the jetty. I looked round but George and his friend had disappeared and the locals carried on their business as if nothing had happened.

'We are looking for the customs office,' I offered by way of an apology, but the police officer was having none of it. They had been called out to a disturbance and were determined to make an arrest. 'Follow us to the police station,' he ordered as he waved his machine gun dangerously close to our faces once again. It was blatantly obvious to me that we had entered Colombia illegally!

It felt good to be straddling *Kate* again and she fired up on the first kick. We were flanked back and front by the police motorcycles and even though the circumstances were a little intimidating, I allowed myself a wry smile as I rode the Norton through the paved streets of Leticia as we were escorted to the police station. We had been cooped up on a boat for nine days and it was great to be riding my motorcycle again albeit only for a half mile or so! Then a loud grinding noise started to come from the chain on my bike but with our armed chaperone in close attendance I had to ignore it and rode on hoping it was nothing too serious.

On every street corner in Leticia I noticed there were groups of soldiers all armed to the teeth. It seemed surreal, but then I reminded myself that we were in Colombia where FARC guerrillas operated freely. It is also the home of some of the biggest drug cartels in the world.

We arrived at the police station and one of the machine gun toting officers ran through the front doors of the garrison building. Within seconds about 30 police officers spilled out onto the street and just stood there staring at us and the bikes. Then the captain of the station pushed his way through his men and introduced himself. There was an uncomfortable silence and it was like a Mexican stand-off. We didn't really know why we were at the police station and the officers and captain didn't seem to know either. So after searching our entire luggage for contraband on the pavement in front of the station, the captain ordered two of his men to escort us to the customs and immigration office to get the necessary stamps and very courteously welcomed us to Colombia.

Although I didn't think about it at the time it was uncanny that Che and Alberto had also entered Colombia illegally via a local man in a small boat and their first port of call was the same police station where our personal belongings had been laid outside on show to all and sundry. The welcome they had received was a little warmer than ours as they were given lodgings at the police station, whereas we would have to find a hostel.

After a couple of hours of form-filling and having a brass rubbing of the Nortons' engine numbers taken, we got our passports stamped and a form allowing us free passage in Colombia for six months. The two friendly policemen who had been our escorts for the afternoon shook our hands, climbed aboard their motorcycle and rode off waving. All we had to do now was find a place to stay

We eventually found a small hostel which had secure parking for the bikes in an empty shop next door to it. While the bikes were parked outside the hostel they drew lots of admiring looks from passers-by and in particular a big American guy who introduced himself as Andy.

Andy was a huge guy from Idaho, an ex semi-pro American football player. Now living in northern Spain, the birthplace of his mother, he was very proud of his Basque heritage and his football career, which had been cut short by a knee injury. He asked us all about our trip and how we were getting the bikes out of Leticia, and after listening to our tale and realising our limited grasp of the Spanish language, Andy offered to translate for us and we arranged to meet him the following morning to go to the local airstrip.

With a population of around 37,000 people, half of whom must have been soldiers and policemen, Leticia was very safe and friendly and we took a brief look round the dusty streets which were full of shops, bars and cafés. We eventually settled ourselves outside a small bar round the corner from our hostel where we shared a large pizza and lots of beer to a background of salsa music, before heading back to the hostel and climbing into the luxury of our beds.

Che and Alberto had spent nine days in Leticia and they eventually left for the capital, Bogotá, by cargo plane. It was the first time Alberto had flown! Without their motorcycle they only had to arrange transport for themselves. We were in a predicament as we had to fly ourselves as well as get the two Nortons to Bogotá in order to carry on our journey following the route of our inspirational predecessors. We hoped Andy could arrange flights quickly as we wanted to get back to travelling via our own mode of transport and not rely on a boat or a plane. The short ride we had taken to the police station had made me realise how much I had missed the day to day riding of *Kate*. I stretched out my legs in my single bed and turned the side light off before going to sleep. I certainly wouldn't miss the swaying nylon cord hammock that was now stowed in my rucksack.

Andy turned up at our hostel at 8 a.m. sharp, clad in a huge Washington Redskins football shirt. We had a quick coffee then set off on the 20-minute walk to the local airstrip. Leaving the main town behind we walked a mile or so before we passed the run-down zoological gardens where a sign on the side of the road boasted snakes, spiders and crocodiles from the Amazon. I looked over the decaying fence of the zoo but all the cages I could see were sadly empty.

Reassuringly, even though we were now well out of the town centre and surrounded by cleared rainforest there were still armed soldiers every couple of hundred yards or so and for all Colombia's reputation, I felt very safe.

Andy quickly went from his American drawl to rapid Spanish as he spoke to the man behind the desk in the small freight office at the airport. Voices were raised and accompanied by the customary waving of hands as Andy tried to explain to the cargo representative that we wanted to fly two motorcycles and ourselves to the capital, Bogotá as soon as possible. After an eternity of discussion Andy turned to us and shook his head as he explained, 'You need police papers, a bank transfer payment for the customs and photocopies of all your documents before he will ship your bikes.' He turned back round to the cargo rep and they exchanged another short burst of machine gun Spanish.

'It will be Tuesday before you can ship them out of here as the police office and the banks are closed until Monday and it will take a day to organise.'

'But it's only Saturday,' Pete replied, the disappointment telling in his voice.

'I'm sorry, but that's the best he can do,' Andy offered by way of an apology.

'The one consolation is that it's the weekend; c'mon lets go and drink some beer,' said Andy, cheering me up immediately. It was only 10.30 a.m. but to me it seemed a great idea and besides we were stuck in Leticia for at least another three days with very little else to do!

We sat outside a small bar in the centre of Leticia and ordered three bottles of Aguila. Pete seemed distant and was mulling round our predicament in his mind, unable to hide his disenchantment at our situation. Andy then suggested that we, 'go to Brazil, where the beer is colder and the bars are busier,' and with that Pete perked up a little. I think this was probably because Che and Alberto had also crossed the open border into the neighbouring town of Tabatinga and then wandered down to the Brazilian harbour. I personally think that the two Argentinians had gone on the lash which was definitely what Andy and I had in mind.

'Brazil is the fourth largest market for beer in the world,' Andy explained as the owner of the bar came over and asked us in Portuguese what we wanted. 'Trés grandes cervejas, Brahma,' Andy responded in Portuguese and before Pete could say 'no' we were served with three large ice cold bottles of Brahma, a strong, local beer.

Looking around us it was as if we had walked into a different world. The Brazilian flag flew proudly from every building and the sound of Brazilian samba music filled the air. Leticia and Tabatinga are basically a town split in half and although they co-operate very closely one half is very rightly proud to be Colombian and the other proudly Brazilian. Different languages are spoken, the cultures are different and even the currency is different as I found out when I paid for the beers with Colombian pesos and was given my change in Brazilian reals. Both sides of the border accept each other's money which was very confusing to me as I now had a mix of notes I didn't know the value of!

We walked down the hill, which was lined with bars, towards the harbour, and managed a cold beer in each one. Pete had by now stopped trying to keep up with me and Andy and he sipped his beer slowly, still deep in thought at the rigmarole we had to go through just to get ourselves and the bikes to Bogotá. Andy was starting to look dishevelled and a little the worse for wear as the strong Brazilian beer kicked in and when we had exhausted the bars near the harbour we walked back up the hill towards the border and a bar that our American friend knew well.

We were greeted at the door by a very attractive Brazilian girl who had perfect white teeth and an angelic smile. She had the most amazing beehive hairstyle which towered above her, somehow managing to defy gravity. Unfortunately, below the neck she had the body of a woolly mammoth. She made the Peruvian riverboat captains look svelte, and her unshaven legs sported a thick thatch of jet black hair. Andy hadn't noticed anything below the sumptuous beauty's neckline. He was captivated by her smouldering looks and babbled to her in an incoherent language that I think he had just made up. He grabbed her hand and pulled her onto his knee as the beer and background samba music set the mood.

We sat down across from Andy and our host and ordered more drinks but Pete was still brooding over our predicament and didn't believe we needed any more papers from the police or customs to carry on our journey through Colombia. He spread the customs papers on the wooden table in front of him and studied them meticulously.

'Steve we must…' but I couldn't hear the rest of the sentence as the music suddenly grew louder and Andy skipped off to dance an amazing fandango with his new friend.

'Steve,' Pete shouted at the top of his voice. 'The customs form allows us free passage in Colombia for six months!' I swallowed my beer and walked over to the fridge to get another but Pete gently grabbed my arm. 'Let's go back to the airstrip and try again,' he pleaded with me. I looked over at Andy but he was so busy tripping the light fantastic that he didn't notice us leaving the bar. We got a motorcycle taxi back over the border to Colombia.

Back at the airstrip we entered the cargo company's offices but the same guy that Andy had spoken to was still there. Fortunately, Pete was very persistent, and after showing him the paperwork and involving a customs officer who was checking some parcels, we were told that we had the right paperwork and could pay in cash to fly the bikes out on Monday morning. To say Pete was elated would be an understatement; his persistence and determination had paid off for both of us. I fear that without it I would still be in that bar in Brazil watching Andy strut his stuff.

Andy looked the worse for wear when he joined us for breakfast on Sunday morning wearing another of his collection of oversized NFL football shirts. He planned to go and spend the rest of the day in bed to shake off his hangover but we had more pressing matters. Bike maintenance!

I spent most of the morning tightening bolts, repairing my panniers and trying to find out what the problem was with my drive chain. Unfortunately, when George and his friends had dropped my bike into his small canoe they had bent the back mudguard, which was now catching against the chain. But after a little persuasion with a pair of vice grips and a hammer I solved the problem and was good to go.

Pete's Norton had a far more serious problem. The gear-box bolts were continually working themselves loose and making it difficult for him to select gears. He had tried to tighten them up but it proved impossible. Pete, being a fully trained precision mechanic, solved the problem methodically after working out the technical strains on the gearbox. Using a hammer he drove another thick wooden wedge into the side of the gearbox which jammed it into place. Then for good measure he wrapped a luggage strap round the gearbox and tied it tightly to the frame of the bike. Pete has a saying, 'If it can't be fixed with cable ties, duct tape or roof rack straps, it's serious.' Obviously he didn't think his gearbox problem too serious!

We rode to Leticia airstrip on the Monday morning at 5.30 a.m. The driving rain soaked us through but failed to dampen our spirits as the two Nortons were weighed on the heavy duty scales and given their cargo labels. We were told that they would fly out later that day or at the latest *mañana* (tomorrow). We were due to fly out on a small passenger jet at 2 p.m. so we sadly parted company with the bikes for only the second time on the trip and headed back to Leticia to grab some breakfast and say our goodbyes to Andy.

It was 3.30 p.m. when the 72-seater Embraer ERJ 145 jet operated by Colombia's Satena Airways finally left the runway with only 17 passengers on board. We were all told to sit in the centre of the aircraft above the wings to help with weight distribution as severe air turbulence started to buffer the aircraft and made for a bumpy flight.

Looking down out of the window of the aircraft I could make out the hundreds of tributaries that carve through the rainforest and feed the Amazon River, which we were now leaving behind us. It was only from above that you truly realised the vastness of the tropical wilderness and the scale of this wonderful continent.

We landed at El Dorado International airport in Bogotá and took a taxi which followed a long highway named Las Americas to a quiet suburb of the city near the United States Embassy, where we managed to find a place to stay. We didn't want to be too far from the airport as we had to pick up the bikes the following morning when we would hopefully be on our way. We ditched our bags at the hostel then went out to find somewhere to eat. There wasn't a soul on the streets but a couple of blocks away there was a bakery and we decided to eat there. On entering the baker's shop we were greeted by a stern-faced armed guard who had a pump action shotgun slung nonchalantly over his shoulder and was gingerly pacing up and down the shop. 'Do not enter Colombia unless your journey is absolutely necessary' had been the advice of our government back home and for the first time I began to think they may have been right, but the freshly baked bread smelt so good that perhaps having an armed guard to prevent it being stolen was the correct precaution to take!

Mañana, was the reply we received when we rang the cargo department at Bogotá airport to see when our motorcycles would arrive. More delays were the last thing we needed and I really wanted to get back to the day to day riding of my bike which I missed so much. After the initial disappointment of realising we wouldn't be carrying on our journey that day, we paid for another night at the hostel then set off to explore.

Bogotá was not at all like I had imagined it would be. It was a vibrant city, which managed to integrate its fast moving modern side with a slower paced cool culture. The tall skyscrapers and shopping malls didn't look at all out of place next to historical buildings which contained numerous museums and libraries. The 'La Candeleria' district totally blew me away. A historic Spanish colonial and baroque neighbourhood in the old city, it houses several universities and gives way to a huge plaza named after Simon Bolivar which is dominated by the beautiful cathedral and civic buildings. The outskirts are littered with unique restaurants and bars and I can only imagine the UK's Foreign Office warning is designed to prevent this gem of a city from being discovered and spoilt by tourists!

The hours passed quickly as we walked round the beautiful streets and I felt an inner warmth I hadn't felt since we had left Buenos Aires. The people were really friendly and welcoming. I even indulged in a spot of gambling on the guinea pig races that were taking place in the square. Yes, in Colombia they race them, back in Peru they eat them!

Mañana was the reply again on Wednesday, as the person at the cargo office which was shipping our bikes from Leticia explained to us that boxes of fish took priority over our motorcycles and that there was simply no room on the cargo plane for our bikes. We rang again on Thursday morning and after being told *manana* yet again we decided to get a taxi to the cargo offices at the airport to find out what the hell was going on.

At the Aerosur cargo desk Pete demanded to know when our bikes would arrive in Bogotá. 'Fish, fish, fish,' was the only answer the clerk could give us as he picked up the telephone, stabbed his stubby fingers at the keypad and chatted away on the handset for a few minutes. He then replaced the receiver and spun round towards us, 'Manana! Manana!' he shouted.

We trudged out of the office without even a protest and returned to the city centre to explore what we had already explored over the last couple of days. I was beginning to feel like a prisoner and wondered if we would ever complete our journey. As beautiful as Bogotá is we had seen all there was to see and after the experience of being stuck aboard the *Tuky*, the situation had a feeling of déjà vu about it!

Thursday passed and then finally on Friday the 13th we called the cargo office to be told the bikes had arrived on the overnight flight. With huge smiles and our heavy bags packed we took a taxi to the airport. We hoped that today we would be riding once again!

Chapter 19
Back in the saddle

Breaking free from the clouds the sun shone brightly as we navigated our way out of Bogotá on a busy three lane highway which would take us deeper into Colombia. It felt fantastic to be riding *Kate* again and once more she drew admiring glances from passing motorists. The last couple of weeks sailing down the river and being cooped up in Leticia and Bogotá waiting for the bikes had really made me appreciate once again the freedom that riding a motorcycle gives you. The sights and the smells of the traffic-filled road were back with us as a big yellow school bus changed lanes unexpectedly, nearly knocking Pete off his bike before leaving us both blind in the cloud of thick black diesel exhaust smoke it left in its wake.

We weaved from lane to lane as the heavy traffic moved very slowly out of the city centre with the usual mix of beeping of horns and Latino impatience. After a couple of miles though the grin was back on my sunburnt face and I gently opened *Kate's* throttle to keep up with Pete as the sweet tune of the Norton's engine reverberated in my ears. Then I saw something snake across the road directly in front of me as Pete's bike suddenly lost all drive and came to a halt at the side of the busy highway. His drive chain had snapped and was left lying behind us in the middle of the busy road. After risking life and limb to retrieve it Pete got his tools out and set about the task of fitting the one spare split link we had to repair the chain. Unfortunately after a little prising and levering the split link quite literally split and we were stranded in a city that didn't seem to want to let us leave!

We had to find a garage and after what seemed like an eternity of pushing the heavily laden motorcycles down the pavement at the side of the highway a couple of friendly locals guided us to a motorcycle repair shop. We just couldn't have made up what followed after that. Pete pointed out the broken chain to the owner of the shop; the proprietor wheeled the Norton into the workshop and fitted a new link and reacquainted the chain with the bike. He then gave us brand new spark plugs, spare cables, spare split links and a T-shirt each, with the name of his bike shop proudly displayed on the back.

'If you need any help while you are in Colombia please call me,' he told us. 'The cost: zero.' He then handed us an ice cold drink each and politely asked if he and his staff could have their photographs taken with the two old campaigners and the Nortons!

We offered payment but he was having none of it. He vigorously shook our hands as we mounted up and said our farewells to him and his staff. Then once again we set off riding in the direction of the *autopista* and hopefully, this time, out of the city of Bogotá.

We were soon on the *autopista* and the road surface was very good apart from one or two dozen manhole covers that were missing. It was early afternoon and we had been warned not to ride at night in Colombia as the FARC guerrillas were active in the area. Thick black clouds had congregated over the mountains we were riding towards but we had to push on and get some miles under our belts. The sun was joined by a light drizzle which created beautiful rainbows on the road ahead. The climatic conditions in the area were very irregular and unpredictable and sunny mornings often gave way to severely storm-lashed afternoons and, unfortunately for us, this was to be one of them!

A rumble of thunder echoed loudly off the mountainsides and it was as if someone had suddenly turned a tap on, as the black clouds now directly above us, shed their heavy load. We were drenched in seconds, my boots and the front pocket of my cagoule quickly filling with rainwater, and the spray off the overtaking trucks and cars making visibility very poor. We had no choice but to ride on and, to make matters worse, as we climbed up the mountain roads the heavy rain turned to hail.

The temperature quickly plummeted and my goggles steamed up, rendering them useless. I couldn't see anything ahead of me so I quickly donned my sunglasses and had to ride peeping down the bridge of my nose over the top of the glasses, while doing my best to shield my eyes from the relentless hailstones with the peak of my crash helmet. It got colder and colder and we should not have been riding in those conditions but there was no stopping as it was far too dangerous. Even the regular manned Army and National Guard checkpoints had been abandoned and we didn't know if this was because of the weather or the FARC guerrillas.

We passed a sign that told us the next town was 100 km away. After a total of four hours driving in rain, near nil visibility and cold, we dropped down a sheer valley road and were greeted by a sign welcoming us to the central Colombian town of Tunja, where immediately we saw a welcoming red neon sign reading 'Hostal'.

From the comfort of my bed I looked down at my rain-sodden riding clothes which were sat in a puddle on the cold stone floor of the dark damp room we had been allocated. It had been our first day's riding in a while and it had been a long, hard day. The cold had once again become our worst foe but Pete was having real problems with his gearbox which was jumping out of gear. Even though he was riding with his foot pressed hard on the gear lever, the constant movement of the gearbox which was now held in place by two chocks of wood was giving us cause for concern.

The following morning Pete spread out his huge map of Colombia which hung over the sides of his shabby single bed. 'Bucaramanga is hopefully next,' he proclaimed as he pointed out the last sizeable city before the border. 'Two days riding in Colombia and two days riding in Venezuela and we should reach Caracas,' he said optimistically.

I felt a little sad as it was only then that I had realised our trip was coming to an end and in possibly four days (if we made it) our adventure would be over. He carefully folded the map back up, placed it in his rucksack and we walked down to the bikes to get an early start.

The early morning sun beat down on us but after yesterday I was taking no chances and donned my waterproofs. I kicked *Kate* into life and after Pete had hammered the wooden wedges hard against his Norton's gearbox and tied it tightly to the frame again with the spare luggage strap, we set off on the ride to Bucaramanga. We skirted past the picturesque town of Tunja as the road climbed back up into the mountains and we started to pass through beautiful villages which all looked like they were entering the 'Bloom of the Year' award for the best kept village. With their red tiled roofs and brightly painted white stone walls they were impeccable and it was only a cowboy on horseback herding his cattle that gave any evidence of bygone times. The road to Bucaramanga was absolutely stunning, with orange groves along the sides of the road and corn and banana plantations on the hillsides. Exquisite churches with tall pointed steeples that looked like they were puncturing the blue skies added to my sense of euphoria as we started to wind sharply down a road that went on for miles and miles and miles!

The hot sun was at its peak but the ride was made pleasurable by the cooling wind in my face as we rode down a steep valley road which swept round some very sharp bends and my foot pegs often scraped on the road giving off sparks. We passed through frequent military road blocks which were now manned by heavily armed soldiers who always waved us through and once again I felt 'as one' with my Norton. Passing motorists waved and gave us the thumbs up and even when we stopped to take a photograph or for Pete to hammer the wooden chocks that were holding his gearbox in place, cars still beeped at us and waved in a very friendly manner. The Colombians reminded me of the Argentinians – they loved motorcycles!

We passed through a small town called Socorro situated on one of the mountainous slopes where the surrounding forest had been cleared and replaced by fields of citrus, coffee and sugar cane that left a delightful bouquet in my nostrils. The steep streets were adorned with graceful palms with the three domes of the imposing cathedral standing proudly in the central square. The road carried on snaking and it wasn't long before we dropped into the deep valley of the Río Fonce and the colonial town of San Gil which bestrides the main road to Bucaramanga. It was very busy and very noisy, and pedestrians waved and smiled as the low throb of the Nortons' engines passed them. Before we knew it, we had entered the outskirts of 'the city of parks', our destination, Bucaramanga!

We rode round the streets in a daze for what felt like an eternity, as cars and trucks seemed to appear from every direction. Eventually, with Pete's ongoing gearbox problems and a desperate need for something to eat we managed to pull up on a side street to take a breather. It was Saturday evening and everybody seemed to be rushing around and we found ourselves in our usual predicament of needing somewhere cheap and nasty to sleep before darkness shrouded us. Then a young lad appeared from nowhere on a moped and pulled up alongside us to admire the motorcycles.

'You need hotel?' he asked us. I nodded at him then looked up above; 'there is a god,' I thought to myself. He smiled and gestured for us to follow him and it wasn't very long before we pulled up outside a small back street hotel where he pointed towards a shutter door that was slightly open. Then without saying a word he smiled once more, waved frantically and was gone before we could even thank him.

The parking area for our bikes was next to the reception desk of the hotel and there, taking pride of place, was a bright green customised Harley Davidson Chopper with its shiny chrome-work glistening. With its beautifully fabricated extended forks at the front, finished off with a Maltese Cross rear light at the back it looked twice the length of the battered Nortons as we parked them up next to it.

I took a cold shower and as it was Saturday night we decided to take a walk down the main street and experience some Colombian food and hospitality. Bucaramanga is vibrant and one of the fastest growing cities in Latin America and there were plenty of café bars and restaurants lining the brightly lit main street to choose from. Staying away from the local delicacy of *hormigas culonas* (flying ants which have their wings and legs removed before being fried) I decided to stick with the roasted chicken and chips even though the waiter kept reassuring me that the fried ants were a powerful aphrodisiac, which sharing a room with Pete, was the last thing that I needed! I grabbed a six-pack of Aguila from a local supermarket and we headed back to the hotel where I watched an Al Pacino film on the ageing portable TV fastened to the wall above me, while Pete studied his soggy map of Colombia.

'We should hopefully make Cúcuta tomorrow Steve,' Pete said, trying to show me the map, but I was lost in the film above me as Tony Montana buried his face in a pile of the white powder which is Colombia's best-known export.

We were up exceptionally early on the Sunday morning as we wanted to make Cúcuta, which is the last major Colombian town and sits on the Colombian/Venezuelan border. Although it was only about 150 km away there was going to be a lot climbing through the Andean foothills and the terrain was said to be very unpredictable.

As we were loading our gear onto the bikes David, the owner of the hotel, turned up to say hello. David was also the owner of the gleaming green Harley Davidson that we were parked next to and he proudly showed us round his prized possession as he told us of the many competition awards it had won. As well as running the hotel we had stayed in, David was also the president of a local chapter of motorcyclists known as 'The Pharisees' and moments later as we were wheeling the bikes out onto the street a couple more chapter members turned up to admire our bikes.

A giant of a man with a long grey pony-tail and huge biceps stood in front of us and for a moment he temporarily blocked out the sunlight. He had the look of a man who could bend six inch nails with his bare hands. He stepped towards us, 'Hello, I am Orlando,

I am the leader of the Renagades motorcycle club,' he explained. His huge hands enveloped mine as he gave me a firm bone crunching handshake. I tried to work out if he had been named after the city of Orlando or the city had been named after him!

Orlando explained to us that many years ago the two rival chapters of what were true 'Hell's Angels', The Pharisees and The Renegades, fought each other violently, but as they had aged the two warring bands had become one group known as 'Harlistas Farseos y Renegados Bucaramanga' and were now great friends. I remembered my father once telling me, 'Stephen, old age is the best form of gelding,' and the way those two conflicting groups had become such good friends seemed to bear that statement out.

David appeared from behind the shutter doors with a couple of trays of beer as more Harley riders turned up and we all enjoyed a liquid breakfast together on the street while they took pictures of our fully laden bikes. Then David wheeled out his pride and joy, the lustrous green Harley Davidson, into the bright morning sunshine and everybody within a ten mile radius got an early morning alarm call as he fired up the beast. You could see the windows in the surrounding houses shaking in their frames as the two cylinder V-twin engine cleared her throat, popped and growled into life. Car alarms in the immediate vicinity cried out in harmony as the airwaves were filled by the roar and 'potato potato' chop of the 88 cubic inches of the Harley's motor. Then he gently revved the throttle and the noise nearly deafened me as he motioned for Pete to sit on the 'hog' and take it for a ride. Believe me he didn't have to ask twice as Pete took the American machine down the street, watched by us and all of the people hanging out of the surrounding windows who had been woken up and were looking out to see what the commotion was.

Then it was my turn and I nervously straddled the throbbing Harley which, in comparison to the Norton I had been riding for the last couple of months, was an absolute animal. He must have been mad to let me have a go on his bike, but I relished the opportunity and pulled in the clutch and selected first gear. The rasp of the engine made my hair stand on end and I gently let out the clutch and took off down the street setting off all the car alarms that had by then reset themselves. The torque of the engine was amazing and anybody in the neighbourhood who was hoping for a Sunday morning snooze must surely have abandoned any hope by now as I ripped the Harley through the surrounding narrow streets.

I pulled up outside the hotel and David took hold of the bike while I dismounted and I was handed another beer. Riding the Harley for those few brief minutes had been exhilarating and I looked over at my Norton which, compared to the award winning Harley, looked quite sorrowful. But I wouldn't have swapped her for any of the other motorcycles on the street. *Kate* had more 'wow' factor than the lot of them put together.

We bade the 'Harlistas' goodbye and as we were about to leave one of the group pointed in worry at the puddle of oil that had formed beneath my bike. I nodded my head and laughed at him reassuringly; I knew it would take far too long to explain in my limited Spanish!

The road out of Bucaramanga climbed and climbed steeply up the mountainsides and the all too familiar *Curva Peligrosa* signs were once again on the edge of every sharp bend. The tree-lined passage became so steep in places I thought we would need to use a ladder to get up the mountains as the Nortons really struggled for pace.

The day had started warm but the temperature began to decline as we ascended and before we knew it we were at cloud level and it was as if someone had turned on a dry ice machine. Visibility suddenly became nil and the biggest worry for us was being taken out by a truck or coach coming the opposite way on the narrow mountain pass. My hands and feet were numb from the cold and I stayed as close as I could behind Pete's bike as he still had a working headlight.

It might seem strange but at the time I probably needed to concentrate on riding the most, I started to daydream. I don't know why I did this, perhaps tiredness, worry, or perhaps the three cans of beer I had drunk for my breakfast? I couldn't see the surrounding forest because of the low cloud but I could smell the dampness of the foliage and it reminded me of home and my mind wandered for a few brief seconds until the bright lights of an oncoming American-style truck on the wrong side of the road brought me to my senses as both Pete and I somehow managed to avoid being hit by riding onto an overhanging ledge at the side of the road. Then, as we neared the pinnacle of the mountain the cloud suddenly disappeared and we came to a toll booth.

Riding through the toll booth we started to descend the mountain quickly and it was as if we had entered a different world. The lushness of the rainforest and green vegetation growing out of every nook and cranny had gone, replaced with a sparse landscape as dull as the grey clouds above, and the road had simply turned into a potholed dirt track. Even the odd remote villages we passed through seemed bland and soulless and nobody waved at the passing Nortons, which was very unusual. Everyone we saw was on horseback and it looked compulsory for the men of the villages to wear a cowboy hat and a black 1980s porn star moustache!

The heavy rain started again but I was prepared for it as the road quickly turned to mud and deep ruts. With the help of the Norton I ploughed my way through it with very little problem. We were dropping down the sierra into a valley as the road wormed its way down the back of the mountain and then a couple of cars appeared behind us and followed us all the way down the winding road to a small town called Pamplona where we stopped for fuel and a bite to eat.

The final few miles to our border destination took a little longer than we expected as the winding road seemed to cut back on itself all the time and it felt like we were riding round in circles.

We finally entered the deserted Colombian city of Cúcuta on Sunday 15th March, at about 2.30 p.m. and hardly saw a soul. My first thought was that as it was Sunday and Colombia was a devout Catholic country, perhaps the majority of the one million people living there were in the twenty or so city churches. It felt eerie to be riding in such a big city with hardly anybody on the streets and we quickly found a place to stay with secure parking called, 'Del Paz'. It was the earliest we had arrived at our destination in a while so we just threw our bags in the room and set off to explore the forlorn city.

We trudged the spartan narrow streets for a good half hour or so but could not find a bar or restaurant that was open. We were just about to go back to our hostel when we came across the reason why. There in front of us, in a huge open space, was the General Santander Stadium, the home of the city's football club, Cúcuta Deportivo who were playing a home game against Atlético Nacional, a team from Medellin.

There were thousands of people clad in the red and black shirt of Deportivo crammed onto the forecourt of the stadium and the atmosphere was electric! The stadium in front of us was a complete sell-out and it seemed as if the whole town had come just to sit outside on the forecourt while listening to the game on small radios. One minute you could hear the 45,000 people inside the stadium cheering or groaning as the action took place in front of them, then seconds later the countless thousands stood outside the stadium echoed their fellow supporters as the game filtered through on their hand-held radios.

I was moved to see the passion the Colombians had for their football; it reminded me so much of our own fervour for the game back in England. The fast food stands bordering the crowd were doing a roaring trade selling sweet breads, cornmeal and meat fritters and the smell lingered tantalisingly in the humid afternoon air. We stood around for a while soaking up the atmosphere and milling among the thousands of supporters who were all willing their team to win.

The game finally finished in a draw and the crowd came flooding out of the stadium and we were suddenly caught up in a tidal wave of people as they started to walk back towards the city. I don't know if the church services finished at the same time, but the streets were swarming with people as intermittent car horns beeped all around. The many bars and restaurants that had earlier appeared to be boarded up or closed suddenly burst into life. It was like somebody had lit the blue touch paper as music and song filled the warm evening and Cúcuta burst into party mode.

The bar we went to was chock-a-block with people and I had to push my way to the bar to order some drinks. The locals were very friendly and welcoming and we enjoyed quite a few beers as the football chants went up a decibel and the dancing started, first on the floor and then on the tables. The owner of the bar, who looked like a Mexican bandit, was a great host who went out of his way to keep us supplied with beer and tequila as we partied on into the small hours before eventually staggering back to the hostel, leaving the celebrations in full swing behind us.

We were to cross the border into Venezuela the following morning and although we had only been in Colombia a few days it had been a wonderful cultural experience and I would genuinely miss the warmth and friendliness of the Colombian party people.

Chapter 20
Si Chavez!

We left Cúcuta at about nine o'clock; we would soon be crossing into Venezuela via the busiest border crossing in the whole of South America. Our final destination of Caracas was about 520 miles away but after what we had experienced over the last few weeks it would have been impossible to put a time scale on how long our journey would take us.

We edged through the narrow streets to a background of noisy radios, which seemed to be blaring out from every household and picked up a sign pointing the way to Venezuela. The traffic was very heavy as it slowly crept towards the busy border and before we knew it we were wedged in among lots of huge 1970s American cars sporting Venezuelan number plates, along with countless buses, trucks and mopeds. The traffic line out of Colombia was a free for all as everybody jostled for a place on the bridge over the Táchira River which separated the border posts of the two countries. We were swept on unknowingly out of Colombia and at the other side of the bridge the impressive customs and immigration building had a huge sign which welcomed us to the 'Bolivarian Republic of Venezuela'.

It seemed that it wouldn't take as long to cross the border as we had anticipated, but on entering the customs building we were in for a shock. The building was large inside and after eventually finding the right window for 'gringos with motorcycles', a young lady demanded our papers without the 'Welcome to Venezuela smile' we had been expecting. 'Your papers are wrong,' she frowned at us. 'You need to be stamped out of Colombia, before you can attempt to enter Venezuela,' and with that she thrust our passports and papers back at us.

It had taken us over half an hour just to cross the bridge spanning the two countries due to the volume of traffic, so we decided to leave the bikes outside the customs office and walk the half mile or so back to Colombia to get our paperwork in order, so that we could enter Venezuela and avoid the lengthening traffic queue.

We entered the office on the Colombian side and showed our documentation to the smiling lady customs officer. 'Everything seems in order,' she told us. 'Where are your motorcycles?' I pointed in the general direction of the busy bridge and came up with the answer she did not want to hear, 'In Venezuela.' I sounded like an idiot and she looked at us, puzzled as to how we were in Colombia and our bikes were in Venezuela.

I explained our predicament and she told us that they needed the bikes there to take a brass rubbing of the frame and engine numbers just like they had when we entered Colombia. She called over a plain clothes customs officer, had a quiet word with him and he started up his scooter and summoned me to get on the back. He pushed a barrier out of the way and I found myself riding pillion on the customs officer's scooter on the wrong side of the road, weaving in and out of oncoming traffic towards Venezuela. It was a hair-raising experience made even more scary by the fact that neither of us had a crash helmet on and I felt very vulnerable as he kicked a couple of the American cars in passing, just to let them know he was there. Thankfully, the bikes were still where we had left them and after taking a rubbing of the engine and frame numbers I got back on his scooter and we headed across the river once more to Colombia.

Our paperwork was soon sorted and the Colombian customs officers and border police kindly gave us some oranges and watermelon which they had purchased from a vendor, then waved us off. We recrossed the bridge over the Táchira River and into Venezuela. I found it strange that on their visit Che and Alberto had found the Colombian people very unhelpful and a little hostile towards them whereas we had found the total opposite. As Alberto put it, 'The customs officers on the Colombian–Venezuelan border reactivated my anti-Colombian allergy.' From my point of view they had reinforced my love of Colombia!

We hoped to get through the Venezuelan checkpoint quickly, so we could push on to the town of Barinas, but first we had to get through the red tape and form-filling that entitled us to enter the land of Bolívar.

The despondent young lady at window three told us that we needed a photocopy of our driving licences, passports and *seguridad* (whatever that was). So leaving the bikes we once again trudged into the small adjoining border town of San Antonio del Táchira to find somewhere to copy our documents.

Back at window three we presented the copies of our driving licences, passports and *seguridad* (which turned out to be insurance) to the young lady who then told us to go and register with immigration while she checked our paperwork. After queuing and filling in numerous forms at window seven (immigration) then queuing and getting them stamped at window eleven (customs and border control), we took the immigration forms back to window three which was now closed for lunch until 1 p.m.

After an extended lunch break which went on until 1.40 p.m. the girl who was dealing with our paperwork took her seat at window three and told us that we needed stamps, which meant another trip into the town of San

Antonio del Táchira. Finally at 3.50 p.m., some six hours after arriving at the customs office, we got our passports stamped and signed allowing us and our motorcycles passage into Venezuela.

'Welcome to Venezuela,' she said with a scowl.

We set off, but within a couple of hundred yards we were stopped at an army checkpoint and asked for our papers and our destination in Venezuela. Then a couple of hundred yards further up the road we were stopped once more, this time at a police checkpoint, where we were asked the same probing questions. My first impressions of the Venezuelans were not very favourable. They seemed miserable and suspicious, which was probably due to the propaganda and anti-Western rhetoric of Chavez's socialist government.

We rode on towards San Cristobel hoping to get there before it got dark. All along the roadside were posters of the president, Hugo Chavez with his campaign message *Si Chavez* scrawled underneath. I presumed there had been recent elections as the slogan *Si Chavez* was everywhere, on lampposts, trees and even painted in bright gloss paint on fallen rocks that littered the roadside. We had lost most of the day crossing the border and were desperate to find a roadside hotel or hostel, when suddenly my Norton failed to respond and slowed up. We had started to climb a steep hill and I suddenly lost all power and came to a halt at the side of the busy road. I could only watch in frustration as Pete disappeared into the distance and I was stranded. I instantly knew what the problem was: my throttle cable had snapped, just like it had back in Chile.

My faith in the Venezuelans was restored when two passing motorcyclists on Harley Davidsons stopped to see if I was okay and then Pete finally returned to see what the problem was. Within ten minutes he had made a repair and looped the cable over my glove so that I could pull the cable by hand and on we rode to San Cristobel. We were getting desperate and needed to find a place to stay as night was falling when a motel, that looked to be closed and was in total darkness, appeared at the side of the road.

'Have you got a room for two people?' I asked the man who eventually answered the door after I had knocked for the fifth time. 'What time are you leaving?' was his rather strange reply, as he opened the door just wide enough for us to enter the dark hallway, before slamming it shut behind us.

Pete and I looked at each other. It was like a scene from one of those horror movies where you are willing people not to enter the house because you know something terrible is going to happen, but they are too stupid to realise it. We slowly followed our host up three flights of concrete stairs. It was obvious we were the only guests for the night as the place was deserted. He opened the door to a room which had two single beds in it and took the key out of the door and put it in his pocket.

'Can we have the key please?' I asked him as I handed over payment for the room.

'I will look after it for you,' he said as he patted the pocket with the key in it and disappeared back down the concrete steps into the darkness. 'Bloody hell Pete, he's a strange one,' I whispered as we both had the same thought and simultaneously jammed our beds firmly behind the door and collapsed on them in a fit of laughter.

I didn't sleep very well that night as the place was so cold and eerie. We wanted to get off to a good start as we had lost a day at the border crossing, so we planned to set off at stupid o'clock the following morning and I spent the whole night looking at my watch so as not to oversleep.

We got out of our beds at six in the morning, and it was still dark as we loaded the bikes up to get on our way. I kicked *Kate* into life and tied the throttle cable round my hand to gently rev her. It was a difficult task at first as when I turned my handlebars to the left it pulled the cable tight and revved the engine far too much and when I turned the bars to the right the cable went slack and there were no revs whatsoever. I had to manage it until we could find somewhere to get it repaired. Pete hammered the wedges of wood which held his gearbox in place and we pulled out onto the busy road and set off in the general direction of Caracas.

Within minutes I saw a familiar 'snake' sliding across the road as Pete's chain came off his bike yet again and I parked up and ran back to retrieve it. It was the same problem as back in Bogotá, the split link had come off. Thankfully we had the spare link the bike shop owner had given us and, as Pete had become something of an expert at fitting one, we were soon back on our way.

The beautiful countryside was once again blemished by thousands of posters and pictures of President Hugo Chavez and even a passing ambulance with posters all over it relayed the message as if we hadn't already got it, *Si Chavez*. Then for about ten miles after that every roadside lamppost and telegraph pole we passed was painted in bright yellow, green and white with a *Vote Juan* logo. The two presidential candidates had vandalised and decimated the landscape with their campaigns and to make matters worse 'Juan' was the leader of the party that had pledged to clean up the environment! The fact that nearly every car we saw was an old gas guzzling V8 American muscle car told the story of who had won the election.

We stopped at a fuel station to fill up, but the petrol attendant didn't even acknowledge me as I greeted him. He simply filled up my bike and spare can and looked at me very suspiciously. The atmosphere was intimidating but I reckoned he was just having a bad day. After Pete had refuelled I walked over to the attendant and asked him how much it was for the fuel? He pointed to the dial on the pump which read five gallons.

'1.4 bolívar' was the abrupt reply. I looked straight at him and smiled, I thought he was finally having a joke with me but his face stayed emotionless and his brown eyes just stared right through me as he repeated, '1.4 bolívar.' My mind was spinning as I worked out how many bolívar there were to the English pound and what he had asked for just could not be right. It had cost us 30 bolívar for two cans of orange back at the border crossing and I didn't want to offend him by giving him 1.4 bolívar. 'How much for the five gallons?' I cautiously asked him again. His brow furrowed and he spoke very slowly, obviously thinking that I didn't understand him. 'One bolívar fuerte and four hundred céntimos' (1.4 bolívar), he slurred the words at me, like I was an imbecile. I handed the 1.4 bolívar to him and he snatched it from my grasp and turned away to fill a V6 Dodge charger that had just screeched up to the pumps. I looked around the garage forecourt in bewilderment. I couldn't believe I was in a country where it was a lot cheaper to drink petrol than it was to drink orange juice!

We sat on the side of the forecourt for a while but the passing Venezuelan motorists seemed to disapprove of us and not once was there a smile or a wave in our direction. We had only been in Venezuela for a day and I felt a great unease with the country and its people; I mean how could anybody be so miserable when you could fill your car up for about 60 English pence?

The landscape could have been anywhere in England and the roads were in great condition so we pushed the Nortons to their limit and after a couple more hours riding I spotted a motorcycle repair shop at the side of the road in a small village and we pulled up immediately outside it. There were three men working on a moped and all of them had the same distinctive 'basin' haircut that their president modelled on his campaign posters. At first they totally ignored me so I asked them in my fluent Spanish if they would sell me a throttle cable. At least that's what I thought I had asked them; from the look of contempt they each gave me you would have thought I'd asked for their mother to be stripped, washed and brought to the *gringo's* tent!

I showed them the throttle cable wrapped tightly round my hand and the icy atmosphere melted a little as they seemed to take an interest in the old Nortons. One of them went over to the counter in the shop and started to pull lots of different cables out of a small drawer and brought them over to the bike. Within no time their inquisitive wives and families were looking over the Nortons as one of the men fitted a new throttle cable to my bike and slowly the Latin American hospitality we had been used to before we entered Venezuela came to the fore. The lads from the shop gave Pete a spare split link for his chain and also gave us a couple of spare cables and, typically of motorcycle enthusiasts in that part of the world, they wouldn't take any payment. I offered to buy them all a beer but once again my words were lost in translation and they ended up buying me a beer in a bar near the bike shop.

We had been riding on and off for about 12 hours as we neared the town of San Carlos which was where we planned to spend the night. It was dark and I stupidly missed the turning for the town centre so we ended up on a dual carriageway heading away from the town. I decided to cut across the sandy central reservation in-between the roads to get back to the side of the carriageway that would take us towards the town centre. I spun off the hard road but suddenly the bike got bogged down and wouldn't grip and she threw me off. I was a little shook up and had learned a valuable lesson about my Norton's capabilities and handling. I quickly picked *Kate* up and we rode into town.

San Carlos is a small agricultural town in the north-west of Venezuela and it looked very dodgy in the darkness. I stopped to ask directions to a hostel and the young man who was getting into his car pointed towards the town centre. 'Up there on the right,' he said. 'And be careful, the streets are dangerous,' he shouted at us as he slammed his car door shut and drove off in the opposite direction. It gave me and Pete a very uncomfortable feeling, but we eventually found the hostel which was surrounded by an eight-foot high railing fence. On entering the electric gates the lady sat in the security lodge smiled and welcomed us to San Carlos. It was the friendliest face we had seen since we had left Colombia.

With only 150 miles to go to Caracas I was quite emotional as I loaded up my Norton in the early morning sunshine. I wheeled her out of the compound and sat and waited for Pete at the side of the road. The last couple of months had been one hell of a hard slog and here we were on the last leg of our epic journey and I felt a little nostalgic. I thought about the last couple of months riding through South America and what we had endured, then as Pete came up next to me I mounted *Kate* and at that moment I knew how a mountaineer must feel scaling the last few yards of a mountain peak to reach the summit. Caracas felt almost within touching distance!

There was a petrol station across the road which had a bakery and café beside it so we fuelled the bikes up (with the cheapest fuel in the world) and fuelled ourselves up too, with lots of freshly baked croissants and coffee. I couldn't believe it but as I looked out of the café window most of the people that were congregated on the busy petrol station forecourt were queuing up to have their photographs taken with the Nortons. Even the girls who were serving in the bakery went out on the forecourt and posed next to the bikes and it added to the excitement of the day when they all stood there and waved us off. I had an extra spring in my step (if that is possible while sat on a motorbike) and my grin factor was at its maximum as we rode side-by-side and left San Carlos on our final push to the capital.

The roads were smooth and wide and it wasn't long before we were riding in the countryside and breathing the warm damp air. The cows in the adjacent fields had a comical look about them, as if their ears had been put on upside down, giving them a slight resemblance to the Disney film character, Bambi. There was a very loud humming noise in the air which seemed to be coming from the overhead electricity pylons and was quite haunting.

We got a few more miles up the road and I thought I saw something fall off Pete's bike. Thinking it was the split link I immediately overtook him and pulled him over to the side of the smooth asphalt road but after taking a quick look at the chain, which was still in one piece, we were back on our way. Then I thought I saw something else come away from the rear end of his bike and suddenly Pete's back wheel locked up and black smoke came from the rear tyre. The bike skidded from side to side and he somehow managed to stay upright as the old Norton came to a shuddering halt.

What had happened was that the chain had once again lost its split link and the drive chain had jammed itself firmly between the rear wheel and the chain guard which was badly damaged. I immediately went back to where I thought I saw the pieces falling off Pete's bike, but after searching for a while only managed to recover part of the link which held the chain together.

The sun was blazing and the heat reflected off the tarmac road. We were in a real predicament and had no spare link except the one we had been given which was the wrong size and we were miles from the nearest town. But Pete refused to be beaten and stripped a length of copper wire and expertly wound it tightly round the link before applying some glue which miraculously held the drive chain firmly together. We then rode on through countless towns and small villages, which had two speed bumps on entering them and two speed bumps on leaving placed next to the police checkpoints, all of which nonchalantly waved us through. The chain was holding up.

Then after a few more miles we passed through a village where a small podgy policeman in full combat gear leapt out of his police control box at the opposite side of the road, blew his whistle and pointed directly at me. I did what I always did at police checkpoints: smiled, waved and carried on. We were only a couple of miles down the road when a Suzuki DR350 in police livery pulled up next to me with two Venezuelan police officers on it and ordered me to pull over. My smiling face hadn't worked this time!

The taller of the two coppers pulled Pete away from the side of the road to ask him for his papers. Unfortunately, I was confronted by the small podgy policeman wearing full combat gear and huge jackboots who had tried to stop me at the last checkpoint we had ridden through. He removed his crash helmet and sun glasses to reveal his 'Chavez' haircut and growling bulldog face. He then proceeded to stab his finger repeatedly into my chest and demanded to see my papers. I handed them over to him and his glaring eyes scoured through them thoroughly. 'No licence, no licence,' he snapped. 'Yes, everything is in order,' I told him as I pointed at my International Driving Licence. But the bastard was having none of it and seemed to be on a mission to make me pay for having the audacity to ride through HIS checkpoint!

The taller officer who had been dealing with Pete didn't seem to have a problem and returned his papers to him and then remounted the police patrol bike, but the one who was confronting me had no intention of letting us go on our way and put my documents into the pocket of his black combat jacket. 'Follow me,' he barked as he drew his pistol from the holster on his belt and waved it at us before mounting the pillion seat of the police bike. We had no choice but to follow the police motorcycle back the few miles to the checkpoint we had passed through, where there were six or seven other officers milling around.

We parked the Nortons up at the side of the police checkpoint and I walked over to where the copper who had my documents stood. The other officers looked totally disinterested in his appeals for them to look at my papers and once more I appealed to him to return them to me. 'Tax, you must pay a tax,' he told me, but I was having none of it. We had been in South America for over two months and it was the first time we had come across a corrupt official trying to extract money from us.

Then what looked like a five star general, who had more medals pinned on his chest than a war veteran, came over towards us to see what all the commotion was about. It was the senior police officer and he demanded my documents from the podgy policeman and after he had inspected them told 'podgy' that the papers were in order and gave them back to me.

The little fat copper was beside himself with rage, having been totally embarrassed in front of his colleagues, and he needed to save face quickly. 'I want to test your motorcycle,' he snarled at me and, even though it was against my better judgement, I reluctantly agreed and started *Kate* to allow him to ride her. He rode her a couple of hundred yards down the road and returned with a smile on his fat face as he passed off jokes to the other officers and handed the Norton back to me. He then told us our papers were fine and we could continue on our way to Caracas.

We pushed the bikes hard, determined to make it, and as we neared the capital the roads were very busy and every passing truck and car seemed to beep their horn at us. The truck drivers were very aggressive and had the knack of undertaking as well as overtaking and it was very scary riding in-between the huge trucks, which had very little regard for our safety. There was a smell of scorched earth in the air because the hot summer weather had taken its toll on the surrounding blackened fields and many grass fires were still burning in the distance, just as they had been back in Argentina when we first embarked on our journey.

We high fived each other as we rode side-by-side past the sign which read 'Bienvenidos a Caracas' and dropped down the hill into the Venezuelan capital. I felt a rush of mixed emotions as we rode into the city centre. Disbelief that we had finally achieved what we set out to do. Relief that we had made it against all the odds. Great sadness that the journey had finally come to an end and a great sense of joy and pride that we had completed the journey for both ourselves, our families and in particular the two young Argentinian men who had pioneered the journey, Dr Ernesto 'Che' Guevara and Dr Alberto Granado.

A giant red coffee cup and a big cola sphere dominated the top of the two tallest buildings in Caracas. For the last time we navigated the two Nortons into a city centre. We found a hotel downtown with secure underground parking for £30 per night. It was a little better than what we were used to on our trip, but we deserved it!

Chapter 21
Cuban reunion

Caracas is the murder capital of the world, a statistic which makes most travellers simply bypass it on their way to see the other amazing natural attractions in Venezuela. Located in a beautiful valley it is separated from the coast and the Caribbean Sea by the impressive Mount Avila, a 2,200 metre high peak that watches over the city.

After showering, Pete and I walked down to the hotel reception where one of the taxi drivers who worked from the hotel introduced himself to us. William was a short guy with shoulder length hair, a boyish charm and a winning smile who told us he was originally from Colombia but had married a Venezuelan girl. I warmed to him as he told us proudly that he had taught himself to speak English from watching old movies – which showed in his accent and delivery of the language! 'Caracas is very danj-erous city,' he told us. 'Be very careful with mon-et, pash-pot and du-als,' he explained with a concerned but reassuring smile on his face that put me at ease and made me laugh. We arranged that William would take us to the airport in his taxi the following morning to sort out the transportation of the Nortons back to England. Then we left the hotel and went out into the warm night air to get something to eat in the daunting city cauldron that is Caracas. We were hassled a couple of times by the police who were patrolling the streets and searched for drugs, and at one point four policemen stood on a street corner demanded money from us, but that appeared to be the norm in Venezuela.

William was true to his word and arrived punctually the following morning. On the way out of the city centre on the overflowing highway to the airport, it was staggering to see the beautiful suburbs quickly change to slum housing which was stacked up on the sheer hillsides. These *barrios* are inhabited by the very poor and poverty stricken and are strictly a no-go area to outsiders due to the very high crime rate. The image of Che Guevara was scrawled in paint on many of the walls of the squatters' settlements; even now after all these years he is still a symbol of hope to the poor and needy of Latin America. The *barrios* are where most of President Hugo Chavez's core supporters live; they depend on the social programmes and free health care provided by the socialist government and the residents are fiercely loyal to him.

We arrived at Maiquetía Simón Bolívar airport but William had no idea where the cargo terminal was. We eventually found it, and after parting with American dollars for the shippers we handed over a wad of cash for the customs officers, who simply split the money between themselves. We were told to have the bikes back at the airport for one o'clock prompt to have them weighed and crated up for the flight to Heathrow.

It finally hit home that our journey was at an end when we rode the bikes to the airport. It would be the last time we would ride the Nortons in South America and I savoured every one of those 30 miles from the city centre to the cargo terminal: the warm air in my face, the smell of the countryside and the sight of the *barrios* perched precariously on every hill and mountainside. I thought back to our first day on the road in Argentina and the expectations and excitement I had felt when setting out on our exodus. That turned to sadness as we arrived at the cargo bay and I parked *Kate* up and drained off what fuel remained in the fuel tank. I looked at her for one last time as a couple of cargo company employees came and wheeled her away into a huge shed to be crated up for her flight home.

I took time out to survey the vast cargo area as it was the place where Che and Alberto parted company in July 1952, with Che flying to Miami in the US before returning to Buenos Aires and Alberto getting a job at the Cabo Blanco Leprosarium in Venezuela. They had arranged to meet up when Guevara fully qualified as a doctor, but it would be eight years before they would shake hands again under very different circumstances outside the Banco Nacional de Cuba in Havana. We got into William's cab and headed away from the airport on the 30-mile journey back to Caracas.

I didn't feel comfortable walking the streets of Caracas, especially at night, and after a night of mayhem outside our hotel, where the police zapped one or two drunks with tazers for no apparent reason, we decided to spend the last couple of nights away from the city. We were just killing time before our flight home and the following day, with the coast to the north and near the airport, we decided to head for the beach.

We bade William a fond farewell as he dropped us in Catia la Mar which is a small town very near the airport on the Caribbean coast of northern Venezuela. The town seemed to be split in two by the nearby airport runway and was a very busy place, where once again the Venezuelans eyed the *gringos* suspiciously. The beach was a litter-strewn polluted mess, patrolled by armed guards carrying AK47 assault rifles to protect the bathers from being robbed. It was certainly a far cry from the beaches I had seen back on my holiday in Cuba.

There wasn't a lot to do in Catia la Mar except drink beer and drink beer! The one highlight of the time we spent there was when we entered a bar on the Saturday afternoon to find an illegal gambling den. The bar owner welcomed us with open arms as we ordered beer after beer and bet on the grainy horse racing images he probably fed to the TV by a video recorder. He was the bookie and seemed to know the winner of every race in advance as he thankfully trousered the bolívar we were staking on the losing horses. We finally staggered out of the place drunk into the bright daylight sun and headed back to our dingy hotel to sleep it off. Only a couple more days and we would be on our way home.

On the Sunday afternoon Pete and I went into the centre of Catia la Mar to grab some lunch and do some shopping. I got out of the taxi on the main street and as I stepped onto the high kerb I tripped and fell. I tried to stick my arm out to grab a nearby palm tree to prevent myself hitting the ground but I immediately felt a searing pain. I knew right away that I had dislocated my shoulder and looked at the smiling face of the president on the *Si Chavez* poster nailed to the tree as I crouched down on my knees and screamed out in pain.

Fortunately a passing police patrol car had seen what had happened to me and gave me and Pete a lift to the nearby naval hospital. But after waiting what seemed like an eternity they told me they couldn't put the shoulder back into place without an X-ray being taken first. Unfortunately the naval hospital didn't have an X-ray machine so I had to take a taxi to a clinic on the other side of town where the staff were very helpful and professional. Once again I found myself in the care of a Cuban doctor and his staff.

Known as the 'Oil for Doctors' programme, Fidel Castro's Cuba provides Venezuela with 31,000 Cuban doctors and training for 40,000 Venezuelan medical personnel, in exchange for Venezuela providing Cuba with 100,000 barrels of oil per day. In total, Cuba provides more medical personnel to the developing world than the top eight economies in the world combined.

Unfortunately, the doctor who attended to me wasn't as gentle as his colleague who had manipulated my shoulder back into place in Cuba. After a little probing and searching he grabbed my limb, twisted it into place and forced my shoulder back into its socket, which was very painful but gave me instant relief. After strapping it up tightly with bandages and a sling I thanked the wonderful medical staff, left the clinic and headed for our hotel to pack for the flight home the following day.

I had very mixed emotions as I looked out across the sunny runway and boarded the plane bound for home. I would miss South America and the South American people but I was looking forward to getting home to my wife, family and friends. Leaving for home felt a little like buying a brand new car: a sense of great excitement at getting the new model, tinged with sadness at letting go of the old one that you have become attached to.

When we arrived at Heathrow I was greeted by my wife who was waiting for me excitedly at arrivals. I turned to Pete and shook his hand firmly as we would be going our separate ways just as Che and Alberto had back in Caracas in 1952. We had shared a lot over the last few weeks, companionship, danger, excitement and a hell of a lot of laughs, but the biggest thing by far we had shared was a great friendship and bond. I watched Pete walk off into the distance and, grasping my wife's hand, turned away. It was the first time Pete and I had been apart since that cold morning back in January when we were setting off on our adventure. And what an adventure it had turned out to be!

Index